The Papertown Paperchase

A Musical Play for Children

David Wood

A SAMUEL FRENCH ACTING EDITION

SAMUEL FRENCH

FOUNDED 1830

SAMUELFRENCH-LONDON.CO.UK
SAMUELFRENCH.COM

ISBN 978-0-573-05032-9

www.samuelfrench-london.co.uk

www.samuelfrench.com

FOR AMATEUR PRODUCTION ENQUIRIES

UNITED KINGDOM AND WORLD EXCLUDING NORTH AMERICA

plays@SamuelFrench-London.co.uk

020 7255 4302/01

Each title is subject to availability from Samuel French,

depending upon country of performance.

THE PAPERTOWN PAPERCHASE

First produced by the Worcester Repertory Company at the Swan Theatre, Worcester on Tuesday, 26th December, 1972, with the following cast of characters:

Chief Firefly	John Cunningham
The Salamander	John Bleasdale
Papertown Crier	Robin Baldwin
Postman	John A. Cooper
Professor Paperback	John Cunningham
Mr Quid	Harry B. Wall
Tishoo	Annette Woollett
Lady Carrier Bag	Joy Ring
Litterbug	David Soames
Spike the Pen	Ian Ricketts
Fireman Silver	Chris Tranchell
Blotch	Roger Mutton
Carbon	Anton Phillips
The Paper Clips	John Cunningham
	Ian Ricketts
	Joy Ring
The Paperweight	John A. Cooper
The Scissors	Robin Baldwin
	Harry B. Wall
Fireflies	Robin Baldwin
	John A. Cooper
	Roger Mutton
	Anton Phillips
	Ian Ricketts
	David Soames
	Chris Tranchell
	Harry B. Wall

Directed by Giles Block
Choreography by Judy Stephens
Designed by Louanne Harvey

Subsequently produced in this rewritten version at Sadler's Wells Theatre, London and on tour by Whirligig Theatre (subsidized by Arts Council Touring) in the autumn of 1984, with the following cast of characters:

Chief Firefly	Colin Wakefield
The Salamander	Paul Aylett
Postman	David Bale
Professor Paperback	Colin Wakefield
Mr Quid	Shaun McKenna
Tishoo	Sophia Winter
Lady Carrier Bag	Shannon Sales
Litterbug	Jane Whittenshaw
Spike the Pen	Graham Christopher
Fireman Silver	Mike Elles
Blotch	Ben Forster
Carbon	Gareth Marks
The Paper Clips	David Bale
	Graham Christopher
	Colin Wakefield
The Paperweight	Shannon Sales
The Scissors	David Bale
	Shaun McKenna
Fireflies	David Bale
	Graham Christopher
	Mike Elles
	Ben Forster
	Shaun McKenna
	Gareth Marks
	Shannon Sales
	Jane Whittenshaw
	Sophia Winter
	David Bevan
	Lisa Bowerman
	Howard Leader

Directed by David Wood
Designed by Susie Caulcutt
Choreography by Sheila Falconer
Music supervized by Peter Pontzen
Musical Director Simon Lowe

CHARACTERS

The Salamander: A sort of dragon who is usually happiest living in fire. He cannot speak.

Chief Firefly: A fly who lives in the Land of Fire.

Postman: An envelope.

Lady Carrier Bag: The Chairperson of the Papertown Council.

Professor Paperback: A book who runs the local bookshop and is also Secretary to the Council.

Mr Quid: A pound note. The local Bank Manager and also the Treasurer of the Council.

Tishoo: A rather timid paper tissue—she is always sneezing.

Fireman Silver: The local fireman, made of silver paper, because silver paper doesn't burn.

Spike the Pen: A pen who is also the Keep Papertown Tidy Man.

Litterbug: An insect who takes great delight in throwing litter around.

Blotch: A thief made of blotting paper. He has one blue ink stain—an old war wound.

Carbon: A forger made of carbon paper.

3 Paper Clips

Paperweight

Scissors 1

Scissors 2

Fireflies

A certain amount of doubling can be used. For instance, Mr Quid, Lady Carrier Bag, Professor Paperback and the Postman are all available to play the Chief Firefly and other Fireflies, the Paper Clips, the Paperweight and Scissors 1 and 2. After the final battle Lady Carrier Bag, Professor Paperback and Mr Quid hastily change back from Fireflies to become their Papertown characters, while the Postman remains a Firefly till the end.

SYNOPSIS OF SCENES

The action of the play passes in Papertown and the Land
of Fire, and the lands that lie between them

ACT I

ACT II

WHIRLIGIG PRODUCTION
CHARACTER BREAKDOWN

The following doubling was used in the Whirligig Theatre production of *The Papertown Paperchase* and is shown here as a guide to smaller companies whose numbers are limited.

Actor 1 (M)   Salamander

Actor 2 (M)   Chief Firefly, Professor Paperback, Paperclip

Actor 3 (M)   Postman, Paperclip, Scissors 1, Firefly (Acts I and II)

Actor 4 (F)   Lady Carrier Bag, Paperweight, Firefly (Acts I and II)

Actor 5 (M)   Mr Quid, Scissors 2, Firefly (Acts I and II)

Actor 6 (F)   Tishoo, Firefly (Act I only)

Actor 7 (M)   Fireman Silver, Firefly (Act I only)

Actor 8 (M)   Spike the Pen, Paperclip, Firefly (Act I only)

Actor 9 (F)   Litterbug, Firefly (Act I only)

Actor 10 (M)   Blotch, Firefly (Act I only)

Actor 11 (M)   Carbon, Firefly (Act I only)

Actor 12 (F)   ASM, Firefly (Acts I and II)
Understudy Actors 4, 6 and 9

Actor 13 (M)   ASM, Firefly (Acts I and II)
Understudy Actors 2, 5, 8 and 11

Actor 14 (M)   ASM, Firefly (Acts I and II)
Understudy Actors 1, 3, 7 and 10

AUTHOR'S NOTE
to the original edition

I have often remarked that playing to children demands pace, sincerity and clarity: especially so in this play. A lot happens, calling on speedy cues and scene changes. For this reason I suggest that all the scenes on the Quest are staged very simply, possibly in different areas of one set. In the original production, between the Paperclip Forest, River Ink and Scissors Gorge scenes, short visits were made back to Papertown. I have cut them as they held up the main action; it is essential to have minimal hold-ups for striking and resetting.

Producers should beware of allowing the fantasy to crowd the reality; the situations are very real and "life-and-death" to the characters, and the danger the Salamander brings to the community should not be played down. It follows that the ambiguous nature of the Salamander is vital; he should be frightening, but simultaneously sympathetic. His relationship with Tishoo should be a complex one, progressing from uncertainty, through teasing and cruelty, towards a genuine affection and trust.

Finally, the arguments and discussions in the play must be clearly expressed, so that the dilemmas the characters face achieve their maximum impact. I hope this does not sound as though I consider the play a profound psychological drama! It should be great fun! But the issues it raises concerning suspicion, trust, fear and uncertainty about the unknown are, I hope, as fascinating for children, when played for real, as they are for adults.

David Wood 1974

AUTHOR'S NOTE
to this revised edition

When Whirligig Theatre offered me the opportunity to direct my own play, several years after I wrote it, I was able to take another close look at it!

I decided to cut a character called The Papertown Crier, who was a newspaper. I was sad to see him go but, quite frankly, he had no dramatic function within the play and actually appeared to hold things up.

In rehearsal, I felt that several scenes were over-written, with characters repeating themselves and generally being too wordy. So I made quite a few cuts.

In performance, I began to feel that the second act was a little long. I don't mean that the running time was too long, simply that it 'felt' too long, and I wanted to build sooner to the climax.

For this reason, I experimented by cutting the Scissors Gorge scene. This certainly helped my production, but I'm sure other productions will not have the same problem. Also, I rather like the scene, and it gives Carbon his 'big moment'. So it is retained as an optional scene in this amended version.

David Wood 1994

MUSICAL NUMBERS

ACT I

1	Bring Forth the Salamander	Fireflies
2	The Test of Fire	Fireflies
3	Papertown	Papertown People
4	I'm Litterbug	Litterbug
5	The Waste-Paper Basket	Spike, Litterbug, Tishoo
5A	The Waste-Paper Basket (Reprise)	Papertown People
6	The Hot Food Trail	Papertown People
6A	The Hot Food Trail (Reprise)	Papertown People
6B	The Waste-Paper Basket (Reprise)	Papertown People
7	If I Go, If I Stay	Spike
7A	If I Go, If I Stay (Continuation)	Tishoo
8	The Papertown Paperchase	Papertown People

ACT II

8A	The Papertown Paperchase (Reprise)	Litterbug
9	The First Clue	Litterbug
9A	The Papertown Paperchase (Reprise)	Fireman Silver, Blotch, Carbon
9B	The First Clue (Reprise)	Audience
10	Burn Me	Tishoo
10A	The Papertown Paperchase (Reprise)	Litterbug
11	I'm Paperweight	Paperweight
11A	The Second Clue	Litterbug
11B	The Second Clue (Reprise)	Audience
11C	Burn It (Reprise)	Tishoo
11D	The Third Clue	Litterbug
11E	The Third Clue (Reprise)	Audience
12	Sleepy Salamander	Tishoo
12A	The Papertown Paperchase (Whispered Reprise)	Litterbug
13	Burn Her (Reprise)	Chief Firefly
14	Salute the Salamander	All

ACT I

Scene 1

The Land of Fire

Music as Fireflies are seen in a ritual line -up. Smoke. In a dominant part of the stage there is a hot red cave, which can be passed through. The Chief Firefly is revealed carrying his burning staff of office; this he bangs ceremonially to commence the official proceedings in a modal chant

Chief Firefly Bring forth the Salamander.

The order echoes along the line of Fireflies (sung chant)

Song 1: Bring Forth the Salamander

Firefly 1 Bring
Firefly 2 Forth
Firefly 3 The
Firefly 4 Sal——
Firefly 5   ——a——
Firefly 6   ——man——
Firefly 7   ——der!
All BRING FORTH THE SALAMANDER !

The Salamander enters. He is a sort of dragon. Although he should look fierce, because any creature of this kind is expected to be frightening, he should be able to gain the audience's sympathy later on, and therefore should look appealing also. He stands formally facing the Chief Firefly

During the next speech, the Fireflies punctuate it with hissing, crackling noises, etc.

Chief Firefly Today is the most important day of a young Salamander's life. Today will determine whether you may stay in the Land of Fire. Pass today's examination and you may stay, fail and you will be banished. Prepare for the Test of Fire.

All The Test of Fire!
Chief Firefly First you must tread the steaming stepping stones.

A row of steaming stepping stones is laid out by the Fireflies

Song 2: The Test of Fire

Fireflies   Can a Salamander stand a
               Test of fire?
               Can a Salamander stand a
               Test of fire?
               If a Salamander can stand the fire
               A Salamander can stay in the Land of Fire.

               Our Land grew from a tiny spark
               From the spark grew a flicker
               From the flicker grew a flame
               And the flame grew higher and higher
               From the flame grew a blaze
               From the blaze grew a conflagration
               Which grew into a nation
               Called the Land of Fire.

               Can a Salamander stand a
               Test of Fire?
               Can a Salamander stand a
               Test of Fire?

*The Salamander walks along the stones, the Fireflies applauding and making
noises of appreciation*

Chief Firefly (*speaking*) Next you must walk through the red hot cave.

The Fireflies lead the Salamander to the cave

Fireflies   Can a Salamander stand a
               Test of Fire?
               Can a Salamander stand a
               Test of Fire?

If a Salamander can stand the fire
A Salamander can stay in the Land of Fire.

We all singe in this scorching place
In the cinders we smoulder
Never burn or turn to ash
Never feel hot, never perspire
For to live in this Land
We must pass this examination

Chief Firefly   Or suffer deportation
All   From the Land of Fire.

Can a Salamander stand a
Test of Fire?
Can a Salamander stand a
Test of Fire?

The Salamander passes through the cave; again the Fireflies applaud and make noises of appreciation

Chief Firefly (*speaking*) Finally, the firebreathing test. You must set fire, with your breath, to these dry branches. Succeed and stay in the Land of Fire.

Fireflies bring in the sticks. As they sing, the Salamander prepares to breathe fire

Fireflies   Can a Salamander stand a
Test of Fire?
Can a Salamander stand a
Test of Fire?
If a Salamander can stand the fire
A Salamander can stay in the Land of Fire.

The Salamander takes a deep breath. He breathes. Nothing happens. There is general concern

Chief Firefly Second attempt.

The Salamander breathes. Nothing happens. Greater concern

Third attempt.

The Salamander prepares

This is your last chance.

The Salamander summons up all his concentration, breathes in, and grimly tries the third time. Nothing happens. The Fireflies gasp in surprise. They chatter to one another in amazement. The Chief Firefly bangs his staff

Enough. Fireflies, leave us.

All the Fireflies dart out, leaving the sad Salamander facing the Chief Firefly

You have failed the Test. Have you an explanation?

The Salamander shakes his head

Do you wish to remain here?

The Salamander nods

Then why have you not passed the Test?

The Salamander shrugs his shoulders

You have been lazy. You have not studied properly.

The Salamander shakes his head in denial

You will be taught a lesson. You must accomplish the following task. Go to Papertown, where all is made of paper, and burn it to the ground. Then and only then may you return.

The Salamander turns and walks away

Chief Firefly Burn down Papertown!

Thunderclap

The Chief Firefly cackles and exits

Music. The Lights begin to change as the Salamander makes up his mind to carry out his task. He sets off (perhaps walking on the spot) as the scene change takes place around him

The Lights fade

SCENE 2

Papertown Square. Morning

The Square is made of a large blotter, with green blotting paper that looks like grass. The pump is in fact an Ink Well. Various buildings, all made of paper, surround the square; they include the Bank, the Bookshop, and the Town Hall. Outside sit two red fire buckets marked "SAND"

The Salamander exits as the scene change finishes (or after the first chorus of the song)

The Lights come up to reveal several characters in frozen positions. These "come to life" during the opening song. They are the Postman, Mr Quid (who stands by the bank), Tishoo and Spike the Pen; off stage, joining in the singing, should be Lady Carrier Bag, Professor Paperback, Fireman Silver, Litterbug, plus Blotch and Carbon and any performing ASMs

Song 3: Papertown

All   Town of paper buildings
                 Town of paper people
                 There's a paper church
                 With a paper steeple
                 Take a peep, look around
                 Welcome to Papertown.

The Postman "comes to life"

Postman (*singing*) I'm the Papertown Postman, I have to cope
                 With parcels and letters, and I'm an envelope.

The music continues

The Postman delivers letters to Mr Quid

Postman Good-morning, Mr Quid.
Mr Quid What's good about it?
Postman Post.
Mr Quid About time.
Postman (*singing*)It's Mr Quid, he runs the bank.
                 With money worries, he's an irritable crank.

All sing. Mid-chorus, the Postman knocks on Professor Paperback's bookshop door

All   Town of paper buildings
                    Town of paper people
                    There's a paper church
                    With a paper steeple
                    Take a peep, look around
                    Welcome to Papertown.

Mr Quid goes into the bank

The music continues

Professor Paperback opens the door of his bookshop. He is eccentric, learned and forgetful

Professor Paperback Ah ! "The morn, in russet mantle clad!"
Postman Who?
Professor Paperback Shakespeare. Morning! What can I do for you?
Postman Parcel.
Professor Paperback Sorry. We don't sell parcels. Only books.
Postman No, no, no. I've got a parcel.
Professor Paperback You lucky thing. (*He starts to go in his door*)
Postman (*stopping him*) For you.
Professor Paperback What?
Postman The parcel is for you.
Professor Paperback Oh. Thank you so much.

Postman (*singing*)   Poor Professor, his mem'ry is sometimes slack.
                          His bookshop's a good shop, and he's a paperback!

Music continues

Professor Paperback Your sack's full today!
Postman Yes. It's nearly all for the Town Hall.
Professor Paperback That'll be on account of the meeting.

Mr Quid enters from the Bank

Mr Quid Hurry up, Paperback. Can't afford to be late for the meeting. Time
is money, you know.
Professor Paperback I'm coming. "Swifter than arrow from Cupid's bow."
Postman Who?
Professor Paperback Shakespeare again.
All (*singing*)   In Papertown this morning, all
                          The members of the Council meet at the Town Hall.

*Professor Paperback and Mr Quid go to the Town Hall. They try the door.
It is locked*

Mr Quid It's locked. What's the time?
Postman Five past nine.
Professor Paperback Who has the keys?
Mr Quid The Chairperson. Lady Carrier Bag.
Postman Here she comes.

*Lady Carrier Bag enters on her bicycle. She is a hearty, county, tweedy
carrier bag*

Lady Carrier Bag What ho? Sorry I'm a trifle late. Have a home-made
toffee.

*During the final section of the song, the Town Hall door is unlocked. Lady
Carrier Bag's bicycle is parked*

All   Take a peep, look around
                          Welcome to Papertown.

As the song ends, Mr Quid, Professor Paperback and Lady Carrier Bag go into the Town Hall. The Postman exits

Music as Tishoo and Spike the Pen "come to life". First, Spike sees some litter and spikes it with his nib, then Tishoo, carrying her shopping, goes to the bookshop, finds the door locked and turns to go. Suddenly she stops and builds up to an enormous sneeze. This makes her drop her shopping. She bends down to pick it up, her back towards Spike

Spike spies Tishoo. She looks not unlike another piece of litter. He goes to spike her. In the nick of time, she straightens up, making Spike fall over

Tishoo Oh!
Spike Ah! I beg your pardon, madam; I thought you were litter.
Tishoo No, I'm Tishoo. (*She builds up to a sneeze*) A — a — atishoo!
Spike Bless you! I'm Spike the Pen, "Keep Papertown Tidy" man. I'm sorry ... (*He stops and listens*)

Litterbug can be heard, off, whistling or "la-la-la"-ing

(*Excitedly*) Quick! (*He pulls Tishoo to a hiding place*)

Litterbug enters

Song 4: I'm Litterbug

Litterbug   I'm Litterbug (*Whistle*)
                       I'm Litterbug (*Whistle*)
                       I haven't a care
                       I leave litter ev'rywhere
                       I diddly dare
                       Throw, throw, throw it
                       Wherever I go.

During the song, he distributes several large pieces of litter

                       Cheese and onion crisp bags
                       Empty cornflake packets
                       Opened envelopes, bus tickets,
                       Tomato skins, potato jackets.

I'm Litterbug (*Whistle*)
I'm Litterbug (*Whistle*)
I haven't a care
I leave litter ev'rywhere
I diddly dare
Throw, throw, throw it
Wherever I go.

Spike emerges from hiding and spikes up some of the litter, unseen by Litterbug

Cardboard plates and egg shells
Litter how I like it
Ice cream cartons and sweet wrappers

Spike And here comes Spike the Pen to spike it!

Litterbug sees Spike, who chases him during the last chorus

Litterbug I'm Litterbug (*Whistle*)
I'm Litterbug (*Whistle*)
I haven't a care
I leave litter ev'rywhere
I diddly dare
Throw, throw, throw it
Wherever I go.

Spike corners Litterbug with his nib, against the Ink Well

(*Speaking*) Aaaah!
Spike Got you!
Litterbug Ooh!
Spike You're a menace.
Litterbug No, I'm not. I'm a litterbug. Let me go.
Spike No. Do you think a pen has nothing better to do than spike up after you? I've got letters to write. And come away from the Ink Well.
Litterbug The Ink Well? (*He gasps with fright and jumps away from it*) Please let me go. I'm only a little Litterbug.
Spike No.
Tishoo (*intervening*) Aren't you being a bit hard on him?
Spike No. I've warned him again and again and every day without fail he goes around spreading his litter—sometimes six nibfuls a day!

Tishoo But maybe that's all a litterbug is able to do.
Litterbug She's right!
Spike I can't help that. He's coming with me to the Town Hall. The Council
can decide what to do with him.
Litterbug Oh please!
Spike And I hope they're harsh.
Tishoo What will they do to him?
Spike Put him in the Waste-Paper Basket.

Litterbug gasps

Song 5: The Waste-Paper Basket

All   There's a place we dread
                           Being sent—we'd rather be dead
                           If you don't know its name don't ask it.

                           But if you've done something wrong
                           Then it won't be very long
                           Before you're thrown into the Waste-Paper Basket.
Spike   Off we go.

Litterbug is very nervous

Tishoo Give him another chance.
Spike Sorry, Tishoo. (*Smiling*) I expect they'll let him off with a warning.
Nice meeting you.

Spike and Litterbug go into the Town Hall

Tishoo stares after them

*A fire siren rings out, making Tishoo jump and drop her shopping again. She
frantically starts picking it up again*

Fireman Silver rushes on

Fireman Silver Clear the streets, clear the streets. Emergency.

*Fireman Silver trips over Tishoo's shopping, knocking it flying again. He
recovers himself and runs to the Town Hall*

(*As he goes*) Danger, danger. Out of the way. Clear the streets.

Tishoo panics. She does not know which way to go. The fire siren stops. Music

The Salamander enters ferociously. He sees Tishoo and advances on her, breathing savagely

Tishoo turns and sees him, probably having been warned by the audience. She screams and tries to escape. He corners her against a building and takes aim. He vehemently breathes on her. She closes her eyes in terror. Nothing happens. The Salamander cannot muster fire. Tishoo, realizing this, manages to escape

Fireman Silver enters

Tishoo rushes into his arms. Together they watch the Salamander make a last desperate effort to breathe fire: he fails and, annoyed with himself, shrugs his shoulders

The Salamander stomps out

Forward to the Town Hall. The Council must be informed.
Tishoo Atishoo! What was it?
Fireman Silver A fiery Salamander. Come on.

Fire siren

As the Lights change and the Town Hall revolves, revealing the interior, Fireman Silver and Tishoo set off round the stage, eventually going behind the Town Hall, ready to enter

Scene 3

The Town Hall Council Chamber

Lady Carrier Bag (Chairperson), Mr Quid (Treasurer), Professor Paperback (Secretary) are sitting listening to Spike the Pen reporting Litterbug who nervously awaits judgement

Lady Carrier Bag This is your last chance, Litterbug. Next time — the Waste-Paper Basket.
Litterbug But a litterbug's born to spread litter. I can't help it.
Lady Carrier Bag Don't argue. We've been jolly decent and if you think ...

Lady Carrier Bag is interrupted by the arrival of Tishoo and Fireman Silver blowing his whistle

Fireman Silver Emergency, emergency, stop everything!
Lady Carrier Bag I beg your pardon?
Fireman Silver Stop everything.
Professor Paperback ⎫ *(together)* ⎧ We've only just started.
Mr Quid ⎭   ⎩ How dare you burst in here un-
                                invited ...
Fireman Silver Emergency. Spike, look after Miss Tishoo. She's had a nasty shock.

Spike the Pen takes care of the quaking Tishoo

Spike Certainly.
Tishoo Atishoo. Thank you.
Fireman Silver Now, Madam Chairman, permission to speak.
Lady Carrier Bag Whether I grant it or not I have a feeling it will make scarce difference.
Fireman Silver There is a Salamander loose in Papertown.

Pause

Lady Carrier Bag Really?
Mr Quid What's a Salamander?
Professor Paperback "A lizard-like animal supposed to live and breathe fire; creature who can endure great heat ..."
Lady Carrier Bag What? Fire?

General consternation

All It must be caught. What can we do? Fire in Papertown? We'll all be burnt! *etc., etc.*

Fireman Silver blows his whistle. Silence

Fireman Silver It is important not to panic.

Litterbug screams

Lady Carrier Bag Yes, indeed. Litterbug, cease that racket! Under the table!

Litterbug goes under the table

Fireman Silver Papertown Council, it is up to you to decide what action should be taken. I should warn the Council that the beast is very fierce. If angered he could well burn Papertown to the ground in seconds—well, minutes.
Lady Carrier Bag This is a frightfully grave situation.
Professor Paperback Think of the damage.
Mr Quid Think of the cost.
Professor Paperback Where is it now?
Tishoo It went in the direction of Paperclip Forest, Professor.

A gasp of horror at the mention of this dreaded place

Professor Paperback I suggest we approach the Salamander with a proposal of peace. Invite him back and find out why he is angry.
Lady Carrier Bag Excellent wheeze. We'll write to him . . .
Spike Could I do that, Madam Chairman?
Lady Carrier Bag Do what?
Spike Write the letter.
Mr Quid How much will it cost?
Spike Nothing. This is an emergency . . .
Mr Quid Done. I agree.
Professor Paperback Where will you get the ink for the letter?
Spike From the Ink Well, of course.
Professor Paperback Please take care, take care. That Ink Well is so mysterious and such a worry.
Spike Rubbish.
Professor Paperback I fancy something very sinister will happen there one day.
Lady Carrier Bag Enough gossiping, thank you. Now, where were we? A letter, to be written by Spike the Pen, composed by . . .

Mr Quid I propose Paperback. It was his idea.

All Hear, hear, *etc.*

Lady Carrier Bag Carried unanimously. Composed by Professor Paperback, and delivered by . . . ? Can I have volunteers? Who will actually deliver the letter into the claws of the Salamander?

Silence. Nobody wants this job. There is a knock on the door. All jump

Come in.

The Postman enters

Postman Good-morning. Second post.

The Postman gives the letters to Professor Paperback, then becomes aware of everybody staring at him. Pause

What's the matter?

Lady Carrier Bag Of course! Why didn't we think of it before?

Sudden activity

Spike dashes outside to get a nibful of ink

Mr Quid and Professor Paperback set out a piece of paper

Spike returns and starts to write

Professor Paperback dictates. Tishoo watches Spike writing. Meanwhile Lady Carrier Bag and Fireman Silver talk to the Postman

Postman. You have the super chance of serving the citizens of your town.

Postman But I do that every day of my life—delivering letters.

Lady Carrier Bag Exactly. You will, however, today, deliver a very special letter.

Fireman Silver To a Very Special Person.

Postman All right. As long as it doesn't take too long. My wife will have the lunch ready soon. What's the address?

Lady Carrier Bag We're not absolutely certain.

Postman What? Then how can I deliver it?

Fireman Silver We know it's somewhere in Paperclip Forest.

Postman Paperclip Forest? (*He gasps and trembles at the mention of the place, but bravely tries to cover up his fear*) That's miles away. And it's enormous.

Lady Carrier Bag You simply go to the Forest and call out until he comes.

Postman Until who comes?

Fireman Silver The Salamander.

All turn, looking for the Postman's reaction

Postman What's the Samalander—er— Semolina?

Professor Paperback "A lizard-like animal supposed to live in and breathe fire; creature . . ."

All Shhhh!!

Too late. The Postman has heard

Postman Fire? (*He is horrified*)

Lady Carrier Bag Only the odd little breath.

Postman What? No. I can't. It's impossible. I'm a married man.

The letter is finished. Mr Quid and Professor Paperback fold it

Mr Quid Of course you can. Anyway it's your duty.

Postman Duty?

Mr Quid Yes. Here is a letter. (*He gives the Postman the letter*) You are the postman—deliver it . . .

Postman I can't.

Mr Quid Or you'll get the sack.

Postman What?

Mr Quid You will be fired.

Postman Ooh! All right. Yes. I'll go. Oh dear.

The Postman exits in a state

Lady Carrier Bag Jolly good luck.

All Hear, hear.

Lady Carrier Bag Papertown is proud of you.

The meeting resumes. Litterbug goes on cheering

Litterbug! Under the table! And you can stay there tomorrow as well.

Litterbug goes grudgingly under the table

Mr Quid Now. What arrangements are we making for when the Salamander arrives?

Professor Paperback Well, I thought tea in the Square—or in the Town Hall —perhaps some cake—I could look up whether Salamanders like cake in my encyclopaedia . . .

Mr Quid No, no, no. You've got it all wrong. Once the Salamander is here we must take him prisoner.

Lady Carrier Bag Nonsense, we've invited him to chat about peace terms.

Mr Quid But the creature is ferocious. I reckon we can't afford to trust him.

Spike I agree. We can't take chances.

Tishoo But—atishoo—that seems very unfair. If the Salamander is coming to talk peace we shouldn't trick him.

Fireman Silver That's true, but on the other hand, he might turn nasty. I think Mr Quid is right.

Lady Carrier Bag Let's take a vote. Those for catching the Salamander?

Spike, Mr Quid, Fireman Silver raise their hands

Mr Quid Come on Paperback, you don't want your bookshop burnt down do you?

Professor Paperback No, but . . . Oh, very well. (*He raises his hand*)

Mr Quid And what about you, Madam Chairman?

Lady Carrier Bag I think it wrong to trick the creature.

Mr Quid Rubbish. It's our duty to protect the citizen's lives and property.

Lady Carrier Bag (*sighing*) I suppose so. (*She raises her hand*) Those against.

Tishoo alone raises her hand

Motion carried. We trap the Salamander. Fireman Silver will take charge of the operation.

Fireman Silver Thank you, Madam Chairman. I suggest we lure it into the town and then catch it.

Lady Carrier Bag Where?

Fireman Silver There's only one place—the Waste-Paper Basket.

Everyone gasps

Litterbug comes out from under the table and sings with the others

Song 5A: The Waste-Paper Basket (Reprise)

All   There's a place we dread
                     Being sent—we'd rather be dead
                     If you don't know its name don't ask it.

                     But if you've done something wrong
                     Then it won't be very long
                     Before you're thrown into the Waste-Paper Basket.

Spike But how do we get the Salamander to the Waste-Paper Basket without him being suspicious?
Mr Quid Good question.
Professor Paperback I know. It breathes fire, so it's bound to like hot food. We simply lay hot food all along the road to the Waste-Paper Basket. The Salamander will eat it, and being so engrossed with his delicious meal, will not expect to be trapped.
Lady Carrier Bag Tiptop. Tishoo and I can prepare it.
Tishoo But I don't really think ...
Lady Carrier Bag Tishoo, we must all pull together.

During the following song, Lady Carrier Bag and Tishoo, helped by the others, prepare hot dishes

Song 6: The Hot Food Trail

Lady Carrier Bag We'll cook hot and pungent appetizing dishes
                     To satisfy the Salamander's wildest wishes.

All   Hurry, hurry.
                     Cook a chicken curry
                     And chilli con carne of course
                     Pour in heaps of pepper
                     Hurry, hurry, hurry
                     And don't forget the Worcester Sauce.

Hurry, hurry,
Cook a mutton curry
With relish and pickle of course
Add a slice of ginger
Hurry, hurry, hurry
And don't forget the Worcester Sauce.

The Hot Food Trail
The Hot Food Trail
The Hot Food Trail
Can save us from disaster
It cannot fail
To catch the Salamander faster.

Hurry, hurry,
Cook a codfish curry
With garlic and mustard of course
Spice it up with spices
Hurry, hurry, hurry
And don't forget the Worcester Sauce.

The Hot Food Trail
The Hot Food Trail
The Hot Food Trail
Can save us from disaster
It cannot fail
To catch the Salamander faster.

The Hot Food Trail.

Litterbug is sent back under the table

All the others exit, laying the trail as they go. Their singing dies away into the distance

The Hot Food Trail
The Hot Food Trail
The Hot Food Trail
The Hot Food Trail ...

The Lights fade

Litterbug exits

SCENE 4

Paperclip Forest

It is quite dark and mysterious. Eerie forest noises are heard

The Postman enters, nervous

Postman (*calling*) Samalander. Samalander. Silly gander! Smelly panda! I have a letter for you. Semolina. (*He looks around, sees nothing*) Ooh I'm exhausted. Never have I spent so much time and energy delivering one letter. I don't believe there ever was a Samalander, and I hate this place. They say all sorts of nasty creatures lurk in Paperclip Forest.(*Frightening forest noise*) Better get going again. My wife will have the dinner ready by now. Just check the route. (*He sits, gets out a map of the Forest and holds it up over his face to study it. His legs are stretched out on the ground in front of him*)

The Salamander enters. He crosses towards the Postman, without seeing him, passes him and exits

The Postman folds up his map, not having noticed anything. The audience should tell him the Salamander has just been there. Dialogue (if necessary):

Postman Did you see anything?
Audience Yes.
Postman What was it?
Audience The Salamander.
Postman Which way?
Audience That way.

He sets off in pursuit. The Salamander enters upstage as the Postman exits. He is clearly hungry, and goes to a tree to look for berries or leaves. The Postman enters walking backwards and moving towards the Salamander

The audience may shout a warning, but the Postman carries on until he and the Salamander bump into each other back to back. Both jump, turn and react. Salamander tries to mime an apology, but the Postman clearly sees it as a vicious attack. In the nick of time he remembers the letter and flings it at the Salamander's feet

The Postman exits at full speed

The Salamander sees the note, picks it up, and wonders what to do with it. He smells it, licks it, shakes it, inquisitive. The audience may tell him to open it and read it. In any case he does so eventually and looks at the writing. He asks the audience to read it out for him; it says "Come to Papertown for tea and talks". He gets the audience to read it a second time. Then just the word "tea". He rubs his stomach

He happily sets off for Papertown. (First in the wrong direction, corrected by the audience)

The Lights fade

SCENE 5

At the Waste-Paper Basket

The large Waste-Paper Basket is made of wicker so that we can see people inside through the bars. It is turned over; the only way to get out of it is for someone to crank a handle, pulling a rope that hoists the whole structure off the ground. Inside the Waste-Paper Basket are Blotch and Carbon, playing cards

Lady Carrier Bag, Professor Paperback, Mr Quid, Fireman Silver, Tishoo and Spike the Pen enter, laying the trail

Song 6A: The Hot Food Trail (Reprise)

All   The Hot Food Trail
                       The Hot Food Trail
                       The Hot Food Trail
                       Can save us from disaster

It cannot fail
To catch the Salamander faster.

The trail is laid. Fireman Silver approaches Lady Carrier Bag

Fireman Silver Permission to release the prisoners in readiness for the capture, your Ladyship.
Lady Carrier Bag Granted, Fireman Silver.

Song 6B: The Waste-Paper Basket (Reprise)

All   Wind the handle around
                         Wind it round ——

Blotch }
Carbon } *(together)* —It's leaving the ground!

All   Such a tiring but worthwhile task, it
                         May save us all from a fate
                         Worse than death if we can bait
                         The Salamander to the Waste-Paper Basket.

During the song Fireman Silver and Mr Quid crank the handle, hoisting the Waste-Paper Basket up in the air and releasing Blotch and Carbon

Mr Quid Blotch the thief. Stand forward.
Blotch Yes, Mr Quid.

Blotch steps forward, guarded by Spike

Mr Quid Carbon, the forger. Stand forward.
Carbon Yes, Mr Quid.

Carbon stands forward. Lady Carrier Bag steps forward to give instructions, as though she were reviewing the troops

Lady Carrier Bag Blotch and Carbon, do not suppose that your release is permanent. You are both notorious criminals and your sentences were long. However, the threat of the Salamander must be regarded by all as a National Emergency.
All Hear, hear.

Lady Carrier Bag If you assist us in our distress we may well reward you.
Mr Quid Not with money.
Lady Carrier Bag Not with money, but with shorter sentences of imprisonment in the Waste-Paper Basket. Will you help?
Blotch } (*together*) It would be a pleasure, your Ladyship.
Carbon }
Lady Carrier Bag Right. Take your orders from Fireman Silver, who is our Commander.
Fireman Silver You two will operate the hoist. When the Salamander appears, happily noshing the Hot Food Trail, you will be in lurk, working the crank handle. When the Salamander is underneath the Waste-Paper Basket you simply ——

Fireman Silver is interrupted by the hysterical arrival of the Postman, screaming at the top of his voice

Postman Aaaaah! Hide, hide, hide! He's coming, he's coming! *etc.*

Fireman Silver looks off stage in the direction from which the Postman came

Spike Did you deliver the letter?
Postman (*nodding maniacally*) Yes. And he tried to attack me. He's on his way now. He's . . .

It is all too much for the Postman. He faints, stiff as a board, into Spike's arms

Fireman Silver Everybody hide. Fast. (*To Blotch and Carbon*) You two stay in lurk.

All hide. Spike drags the Postman to safety. Blotch and Carbon nervously stand by the crank handle. Fireman Silver has his buckets at the ready. (Tension music)

The Salamander enters cheerfully, happily eating the Hot Food Trail, and reacting with pleasure to the hot dishes

The Audience may warn him not to go under the Waste-Paper Basket, but he does not hear them. As he reaches the Waste-Paper Basket he realizes he has had enough to eat, and turns back. The other characters emerge in anxious dismay. Fireman Silver has an idea. He starts wafting the smell of a tempting dish in the Salamander's direction. The others carry on "the waft", and just as the Salamander is about to exit, he catches the delicious aroma. It turns

him round; he cannot resist following it back to the dish right under the
Waste-Paper Basket. Fireman Silver shouts the order

Now!

Blotch and Carbon release the Waste-Paper Basket which falls over the
Salamander, trapping him inside. He is naturally very startled and fright-
ened and starts "snarling" ferociously. He pushes his head, or part of it,
through the bars. Spike threatens him with his nib as Fireman Silver, aided
by Blotch and Carbon, tie a large handkerchief or scarf round his mouth and
nose to stop him being able to breathe fire. Tishoo is disturbed by this and
takes no part in it. Lady Carrier Bag is clearly nervous about the situation
also. The Salamander calms down

The prisoner is ready to be addressed, your Ladyship.
Lady Carrier Bag Er—thank you. (*She gingerly goes up to the "bars"*)
Now, Mr Salamander. First of all, I want to say Welcome to Papertown.

Reaction against this statement from Spike and Mr Quid

We are grateful to you for trekking all this way, and feel sure we can,
through discussion and friendly negotiation, arrive at a peaceful solution
to——
Mr Quid Oh for heaven's sake. (*Shaking the bars*) What do you think you're
up to, Salamander? Eh? How dare you try to burn our town.
Tishoo Please, Mr Quid. That's no way to talk to him. (*She gingerly takes off
the scarf. To the Salamander*) Salamander, do you understand me?

The Salamander nods

Where do you come from? Try to explain.

The Salamander mimes "heat". The Audience may shout out the answer

What's he doing? Hot? Heat? (*To the audience*) Where does he come
from?
Audience The Land of Fire.
Tishoo Is that right? The Land of Fire?

The Salamander nods

He comes from the Land of Fire.

Mr Quid He'd better go back there sharpish, I say.

Tishoo Shh. Salamander. Are you willing to go back to the Land of Fire?

The Salamander mimes that he is—but that he cannot

Professor Paperback He is! He isn't!

The Salamander repeats the mime

Tishoo He is. *But he can't.* Is that right?

The Salamander nods

Lady Carrier Bag Why not?

Tishoo Why can't you?

The Salamander mimes firebreathing and fire breaking out. Helped by the audience, the others begin to understand

Tishoo Breathe fire ... Papertown ... You can't return until you've burned down Papertown?

The Salamander nods

I see.

Mr Quid So he *does* want to set fire to us all.

Spike What a nerve.

Professor Paperback But what can we do to help the problem?

Mr Quid I know. Here, Salamander, how much do you want? (*He brandishes money in front of him*) You can have as much as you like, within reason.

The Salamander shakes his head

Tishoo Mr Quid, you can't buy him like that. It seems to me the Salamander needs our sympathy.

Mr Quid }
                  (*together*) Sympathy?
Spike

Fireman Silver (*who has been listening*) Permission to speak, your Ladyship.

Lady Carrier Bag Granted.
Fireman Silver I agree with Miss Tishoo on this. (*To the Salamander*) You
don't want to burn us down, do you?

The Salamander shakes his head

But if you don't, you won't be allowed home? Right?

The Salamander nods

Oh dear. Then what are we to do?
Spike Keep him locked up.

The Salamander reacts angrily

Mr Quid Hear, hear.
Tishoo But why? If he doesn't *want* to burn us down . . .
Fireman Silver Yes, but he *has* to.
Lady Carrier Bag What do you suggest, Fireman Silver?
Fireman Silver I suggest we leave him locked up overnight—under constant
guard. Then tomorrow we will talk to him again.

*The Salamander suddenly shows his ferocity. All scatter. Fireman Silver
shouts out his orders*

Blotch, Carbon, stay on guard duty.
Carbon Yes, Fireman Silver.
Fireman Silver Everybody else, please go home, for your own sakes.
Lady Carrier Bag Blotch and Carbon, we depend on you.
Carbon Thank you, Lady Carrier Bag.

Lady Carrier Bag exits

Professor Paperback Oh dear, the Salamander really does have a point of
view.
Mr Quid Nonsense. You can't go round destroying other people's property.

Mr Quid and Professor Paperback exit

Fireman Silver Blotch and Carbon.

Carbon Yes, Fireman Silver.
Fireman Silver Any trouble, ring the alarm bell.
Carbon Yes, Fireman Silver.

The Salamander has calmed down. Spike attempts to prod him with his nib; Tishoo restrains him

Fireman Silver exits, leaving the buckets in an accessible place

Tishoo Spike, please.
Spike Teach him a lesson.
Tishoo That won't help in the least. He has a point of view—the Professor was right.
Spike You're too soft.
Tishoo I'm not—atishoo. And even if I am, is that bad?
Spike No. I'm not criticizing you. I admire you for it.
Tishoo (*sincerely*) Thank you.
Spike Take care.
Tishoo I will.

Spike exits

Tishoo watches Spike go—confused by her mixed feelings about him. Then she looks at the Salamander in his prison. He waves

Tishoo waves back at the Salamander, then exits

Blotch and Carbon are alone with the Salamander. The Lights begin to fade as dusk approaches. The Salamander slowly falls asleep

Blotch (*imitating Carbon*) Yes, Fireman Silver. Thank you, Lady Carrier Bag. Three bags full, Fireman Silver.
Carbon Shut up and keep guard.
Blotch Since when have I taken orders from you?
Carbon Shut up or I'll throw you down the Ink Well.
Blotch (*really frightened*) The Ink Well? You wouldn't dare.
Carbon Ha, ha, thought that would calm you down.
Blotch Don't make jokes like that. I nearly died at that Ink Well. You can still see my wound.
Carbon All right. I'm sorry. All I'm saying is that if we behave and play it their way, we'll be set free.

Blotch We're free now. (*Doing a little dance*) Free, free, free as the air, free
   as——
Carbon Come back here and stop larking about.
Blotch Spoil sport. (*With sudden vehemence*) And don't tell me what to do!
Carbon Shhhh.
Blotch (*shouting*) I will *not* Shhhh.
Carbon Shhhh.
Blotch Shhhh yourself.
Carbon Look. The Salamander's asleep.
Blotch Lucky old him. (*He yawns*)
Carbon We'll guard him in shifts.
Blotch What?
Carbon We'll guard him in shifts.
Blotch I never wear them.
Carbon Wear what?
Blotch Shifts—they're for ladies.
Carbon No, no, no. You'll guard him while I sleep and vice versa.
Blotch Ah. Right.
Carbon Good-night. Wake me in an hour's time. And don't drop off. (*He
   goes to sleep*)
Blotch Don't drop off. (*He yawns*) Don't drop off. Off don't drop. Don't off
   drop. (*He nods off, then wakes suddenly*) Ont rop doff. Ront op droff. Fop
   Font Foff. (*He nods off, then wakes suddenly*) Dront cough drop. Droff cop
   won't. Wop Woof Woof Woof Woof . . . (*He falls asleep*)

   *There is a pause, then Tishoo enters surreptitiously, carrying a plate of
   food*

   *Tishoo checks that both Blotch and Carbon are asleep, then goes to the bars
   of the Waste-Paper Basket. She tries to pass the plate between the bars
   without waking up the Salamander. She manages this, but her arm is not long
   enough to put it down on the "floor". She has to drop it a few inches. This
   naturally makes a sound. The Salamander wakes and sees her and the plate
   of food. He beckons her over. She tentatively goes to him. He mimes a thank
   you for the food and starts to eat it*

Tishoo (*whispering*) Is it all right?

   The Salamander mimes his approval and appreciation

Good. I'm sorry you're locked in here. But the others all seem to think it's for the best. Atishoo.

The Salamander shakes the bars ferociously

Stop it. You'll wake them up and get me into trouble.

The Salamander immediately stops and mimes an apology

You're sorry?

The Salamander nods . He suddenly points off into the distance

What? Go away? All right, I will.

The Salamander stops her and tries the mime again

You want to go away? I know, but you can't. It's too much of a risk.

The Salamander pleads

But if I let you out, I'll get into serious trouble.

The Salamander mimes that he will go a long way

What? You'll go a long way away? (*He nods*) And not try to burn us down? (*He nods*) You promise? (*He nods*) Well . . .

The audience could be encouraged to help Tishoo decide whether to let him out or not

All right. I'll do it.

The Salamander reacts joyfully, jumping up and down

Shhhh!

He stops

Now . . .

Tishoo goes to the crank handle and with great difficulty turns it. The Waste-Paper Basket is hoisted just enough for the Salamander to crawl out from underneath. With relief Tishoo emits a loud sneeze. Both look over towards Blotch and Carbon. Carbon wakes up, and catches sight of Tishoo pushing the Salamander off and away

The Salamander exits UL

Carbon rings the alarm bell, waking up Blotch, who falls over

Carbon runs off after the Salamander. Blotch, realizing what has happened, rushes off after Carbon. Tishoo dithers, then wisely exits DR

Chase—to music

1 *Fireman Silver enters* UR *and Spike enters* DL. *They meet, see that the Waste-Paper Basket is empty, react and chase off. Fireman Silver exits* UL, *Spike exits* DR

2 *The Salamander enters* DL, *pursued by Blotch and Carbon. They exit* UR

3 *Lady Carrier Bag and Professor Paperback enter,* DR, *Mr Quid enters* UL. *All meet, see the Waste-Paper Basket is empty, decide to give chase, and run off: Lady Carrier Bag and Professor Paperback exit* DL, *Mr Quid exits* UR

4 *The terrified Blotch and Carbon enter* DR, *pursued by the Salamander. They all exit* UL

5 *Tishoo enters nervously* UR. *She goes to the Waste-Paper Basket to retrieve her plate. Spike enters from* DR *and Fireman Silver from* DL. *They meet the startled Tishoo and ask if she has seen the Salamander. She points off* DR, *and Spike and Fireman Silver exit* DR. *Hearing others approaching, Tishoo exits* DL

6 *Lady Carrier Bag enters with Professor Paperback* UL: *Mr Quid enters* DR. *They meet and exchange looks of frustration and lack of success. As they arrive* C, *Blotch enters* DL *pursued by the Salamander, with Carbon bringing up the rear. Blotch and the Salamander exit* DR, *unseen by the group* C. *Carbon spots the group, stops, and tells them that Tishoo set the Salamander free. Yelling "Tishoo, Tishoo", they all exit* UL *in search of her*

7 *Spike and Fireman Silver enter* UR, *and at the same time the Postman enters* DL. *They meet* C, *and the Postman is informed of the situation. As they talk, Blotch, pursued by the Salamander, enters* DR *and exits* DL. *The Salamander sees the group* C, *changes his course and exits* DR. *Spike, Fireman Silver and the Postman see him and exit* DR *in pursuit*

8 *Tishoo enters* UL *and goes to collect her plate from the Waste-Paper Basket. As she does so, Lady Carrier Bag, Professor Paperback, Mr Quid, and Carbon come from* DL. *They cross towards the exit* DR. *Tishoo, seeing them, attempts to exit unseen* DL *but Carbon, at the back of the line, spots her and taps the person in front on the shoulder. The tap goes swiftly down the line; all turn on the spot and chase Tishoo off* DL

9 *Litterbug, unconcerned and spreading litter, enters* UR. *He has to avoid being knocked over by Blotch, who runs on* DL *and exits* DR. *As soon as he has recovered from this shock, Litterbug has to suffer another. From* UR *Spike enters, followed by Fireman Silver and the Postman. Lady Carrier Bag enters* DL, *with Professor Paperback, Mr Quid, and Carbon. The characters in their two lines intersect one another and exit: Spike's line exits* DL, *Lady Carrier Bag's line exits* UR

10 *Litterbug retires to safety at the back, and watches the next event unseen by anybody. Tishoo enters* UL, *looking off* L *nervously. The Salamander enters* DR, *looking off* R *nervously. They collide* C *back to back, and jump. They start to run off, but suddenly the Salamander picks up Tishoo in a fireman's lift and carries her off, screaming,* DR

11 *Blotch enters* UR *and stands* C, *confused and unsure where to go next. Spike, Fireman Silver and the Postman enter* DL. *Lady Carrier Bag, Professor Paperback, Mr Quid, and Carbon enter* DR. *Both lines bump into Blotch, concertina, and everybody falls over. Litterbug comes forward laughing, as they all rise with as much dignity as they can muster*

Spike		Where is he? Where's the
Fireman Silver	*(together: to Litterbug)*	Salamander? Have you seen
Postman		the Salamander pass this
Blotch		way? *etc.*

Lady Carrier Bag ⎤
Professor Paperback ⎬ (*together: to Litterbug*) ⎰ Where's Tishoo? Where
Mr Quid ⎪ is she? The traitress,
Carbon ⎦ have you seen her?
Litterbug (*yelling*) Quiet!

The others react and fall silent

Ladies and gentlemen, please! Who are you looking for?
Spike ⎤
Fireman Silver ⎬ (*together*) The Salamander!
Postman ⎪
Blotch ⎦
⎬ (*together*)
Lady Carrier Bag ⎤
Professor Paperback ⎬ (*together*) Tishoo!
Mr Quid ⎪
Carbon ⎦
Litterbug Please, one at a time. (*He looks at Spike's group*)
Spike ⎤
Fireman Silver ⎬ (*together*) Tishoo!
Postman ⎪
Blotch ⎦

Litterbug looks at Lady Carrier Bag's group

Lady Carrier Bag ⎤
Professor Paperback ⎬ (*together*) The Salamander!
Mr Quid ⎪
Carbon ⎦
Spike Tishoo, why Tishoo?
Mr Quid She's a traitor!
Spike Why?
Mr Quid She let the Salamander out of the Waste-Paper Basket. My word,
    this could cost us a fortune.
Spike (*to Lady Carrier Bag*) Is this true?
Lady Carrier Bag I certainly hope not. I trusted that young gel.
Carbon Sorry, but I saw it with my own eyes.
Blotch Me too. Carbon rang the alarm and off she ran.

Professor Paperback Oh dear. She certainly did look a little guilty. Still,
"the quality of mercy is not strained . . ."
Postman Who?
Professor Paperback Shakespeare.
Litterbug Please, please. Let me tell you. I have just seen the Salamander
heading out of Papertown with Miss Tishoo slung over his back.

All gasp. Silence

Mr Quid (*eventually*) I hope that's the last we see of the pair of them.
Lady Carrier Bag That sounds rather uncharitable.
Spike Rather uncharitable? Listen. She's out there alone with a monster.
Postman Rather her than me.
Mr Quid Serve her right.
Spike She must be rescued. Come on!

Nobody moves

   Fireman Silver?
Fireman Silver Apologies, Spike, but my duty is here.
Spike Somebody? Anybody?

They all turn their backs on Spike

Song 7: If I Go, If I Stay

Spike   If I go, if I stay
                     Will it make any diff'rence either way?
                     If I go, could I save her?
                     Wouldn't that be braver?
                     If I stay, will she suffer?
                     Who can say?
                     They all think she deserves it because she let us down
                     So I must choose between Tishoo and Papertown
                     Should I go, should I stay?
                     Should I go, should I stay?

Spike makes a decision and exits resolutely towards Paperclip Forest

The music continues

The Lights fade

SCENE 6

Paperclip Forest

The Salamander carries on Tishoo, who is sobbing. He drops her, showing that he too is tired. He tries to quieten her. When he fails, he becomes angry with her, which makes her worse. He mimes to her to stay there and, clearly hungry, goes behind a tree searching for food. Tishoo stands and considers escape.

Song 7A: If I Go, If I Stay (Continuation)

Tishoo   If I go, if I stay,
                 Will it make any diff'rence either way?
                 If I go, running blindly,
                 Will he try to find me?
                 If I stay, will he hurt me? I don't know.
                 If I stay here with him can I save Papertown?
                 If I go will he follow and burn us down?
                 Should I stay, should I go?
                 Should I stay, should I go?

Spike the Pen enters

Spike Tishoo!
Tishoo Spike.

The Salamander returns and intervenes

   Go home.
Spike Not unless you come with me. (*To the Salamander*) Let her go.

The Salamander shakes his head

   If you don't, I'll come and take her.

Spike moves forward. The Salamander immediately starts taking deep firebreathing breaths, aiming towards Spike

Tishoo Atishoo. Please, Spike, go away for *my* sake. Go home. I'll be all right.

Spike reluctantly turns and exits

The Salamander picks up Tishoo and carries her off

The Lights fade to Black-out

The Music builds, then leads into ...

SCENE 7

At the Waste-Paper Basket

All are frozen with their backs to the audience as at the end of Scene 5

Spike the Pen enters

Spike The Salamander's got Tishoo! In Paperclip Forest! Please, we must do something!

Professor Paperback I know! A quest!

Mr Quid What's a quest?

Lady Carrier Bag Oh, Mr Quid, come. It's where a small band of stout fellows set off in search of the creature.

Professor Paperback That's right, Lady Carrier Bag. A quest to find the Salamander and take him back to the Land of Fire.

Lady Carrier Bag But the Land of Fire won't admit him unless he has burnt down Papertown.

Professor Paperback We — er — tell a little fib.

Mr Quid I agree. Sounds cheap.

Spike I agree. As long as Tishoo is rescued.

Mr Quid Hang on. Who's going on this quest?

Silence. They all look from one to another

Professor Paperback Got it! This assignment smacks of danger — the danger of fire. Now, what is the only kind of paper that does not burn?

The audience should be given the opportunity to shout out the answer. If not, the other characters should "fail" to answer

Silver! Silver paper! Therefore who should lead the quest?
All Fireman Silver!
Fireman Silver (*joining the others*) Certainly, Councillors. I request two assistants, Blotch and Carbon, to assist me.
Lady Carrier Bag Granted.

Blotch and Carbon approach and stand behind Fireman Silver

Fireman Silver Permission to speak, Madam Chairman.
Lady Carrier Bag Granted.
Fireman Silver Not wishing to be difficult, Madam Chairman, your Ladyship, but would it not be wise to employ someone to follow the tracks?
Lady Carrier Bag How do you mean?
Fireman Silver Well, in order to discover the Salamander with the maximum efficiency, I need someone to sniff him out, follow the tracks and let me know where he is.
Professor Paperback Splendid idea.
Mr Quid How much will it cost?

Litterbug, still in the corner, turns

Litterbug I'm good at sniffing!
Lady Carrier Bag Quiet, Litterbug, don't interrupt.

Litterbug turns away

Mr Quid We can't afford it.
Fireman Silver Pardon me, sir, but it will cost you less in the long run.

Litterbug turns round again

Litterbug I can follow tracks!
Lady Carrier Bag Litterbug, behave!
Professor Paperback How will this fellow let you know where the Salamander is?
Fireman Silver Oh. He'll mark the trees with crosses ——

Litterbug throws handfuls of litter up in the air

— or make signs on the ground ——

They all become riveted by the litter, closely following its progress into the air and down to the ground

— or ... of course! A paperchase! Litterbug can lead ——

All A paperchase!

Song 8: The Papertown Paperchase

(*Singing*)   From Papertown
Via Paperclip Forest
Towards the Land of Fire
The paper people race
Through cavernous chasm and crater
River, ravine and abyss
Through furrow and hedgerow and hollow
We follow
This
Papertown Paperchase.

Papertown people race
On the Papertown Paperchase
Papertown must be free
For Papertown people like you and me
Papertown people like you and me.

From Papertown
Via Paperclip Forest
Towards the Land of Fire
The paper people race
Through cavernous chasm and crater
River, ravine and abyss
Through furrow and hedgerow and hollow
We follow
This
Papertown Paperchase.

	Litterbug sets the pace
	Of the Papertown Paperchase
Litterbug	Litter clues I will lay
	So Papertown people can find the way
All	Papertown people can find the way.

From Papertown
Via Paperclip Forest
Towards the Land of Fire
The paper people race
Through cavernous chasm and crater
River, ravine and abyss
Through furrow and hedgerow and hollow
We follow
This
Papertown Paperchase

**All (except
Fireman Silver
Blotch
Carbon)**

Fireman Silver Carbon and Blotch
Good luck on your quest
We wish you,
For hazards and danger we beg you watch

Spike

And do your best
To save Tishoo.

All

From Papertown
Via Paperclip Forest
Towards the Land of Fire
The paper people race
Through cavernous chasm and crater
River, ravine and abyss
Through furrow and hedgerow and hollow
We follow
This
Papertown, Papertown, Papertown, Papertown, Paper-
town Paperchase.

During the song, Litterbug is welcomed into the quest by the Council. All get ready to go. As the quest begins——

——the CURTAIN *falls*

ACT II

SCENE 1

Paperclip Forest

There are three trees in this eerie forest, through which Litterbug comes, excitedly laying his paperchase, and following tracks

Song 8A: The Papertown Paperchase (Reprise)

Litterbug (*unaccompanied*) Through cavernous chasm and crater
River, ravine and abyss
Through furrow and hedgerow and hollow
We follow
This
Papertown Paperchase.
(*Speaking*) Ooh. Paperclip Forest. Isn't it spooky? Gives me a funny feeling in my tummy. There's a terrible legend about Paperclip Forest. Something to do with the trees. No-one quite understands what it's all about, but people have been known to enter Paperclip Forest and never be seen again. I think I'll go—now the tracks go in that direction. (*He starts to go, then stops suddenly*) Hey, I've got an idea. Fireman Silver will be here soon, following the paperchase. I'd better leave him a message to warn him about this place. (*He vainly looks around for someone to leave a message with*) No-one here. I *can't* leave a message with *nobody*.

The Audience will probably offer to give the message

Would you give it to him for me? Oh, thank you. Now let me see—I know!

Song 9: The First Clue

(*Singing*) Beware, beware,
Take great care

Ev'ry tree
Has a dang'rous mystery.

*Litterbug rehearses the Audience in the song, making sure they always wait
for a "one, two, three" before starting*

That's great. I must go now. Don't forget. You all have to sing together,
otherwise Fireman Silver won't understand. So wait for him to say "one,
two, three". Thank you. Good luck.

*Music. Litterbug exits, scattering paper again. Voices sing off, as Fireman
Silver, Blotch and Carbon arrive, picking up the paper as they follow the
trail*

Song 9A: The Papertown Paperchase (Reprise)

Fireman Silver,   From Papertown
Blotch and   Via Paperclip Forest
Carbon   Towards the Land of Fire
                     The paper people race
                     Through cavernous chasm and crater
                     River, ravine and abyss
                     Through furrow and hedgerow and hollow
                     We follow
                     This
                     Papertown Paperchase.
Fireman Silver (*speaking*) Salamander Search Party, halt!

All stop

Carbon Where are we?
Fireman Silver This must be Paperclip Forest.
Blotch I'm scared. My knees have gone all knobbly — I mean wobbly.
Fireman Silver Pull yourself together, man.
Blotch I can't. Look at those funny trees. They look magic.
Carbon I like magic. That's how I started on the road to being a forger, doing
    magic.
Blotch Well, those trees look magic to me. I'm scared.
Fireman Silver They do look different from the others. How many are there?
All (*counting*) One, two, three.

A deliberate count leads the audience into the message

Song 9B: The First Clue (Reprise)

Audience (*singing*) Beware, beware.
                Take great care
                Ev'ry tree
                Has a dang'rous mystery

Fireman Silver, Blotch and Carbon react, surprised, to hear the Audience sing

Fireman Silver What was that all about ?
Carbon I don't know, they all started singing when we said . . .
All One, two, three.
Audience (*singing*) Beware, beware
                Take great care
                Ev'ry tree
                Has a dang'rous mystery
Fireman Silver Thank you. What was that? A message? Who from?
    Litterbug? Ah. Well I think he's playing a silly game. Those trees are
    nothing to be frightened of.
Blotch Then why are my knees all wobbly?
Carbon (*looking down in surprise*) And mine!
Fireman Silver Nonsense.

*Fireman Silver's knees start shaking and Blotch and Carbon point to them.
He looks down. At this moment the trees start moving down towards them.
The Audience will shout a warning. Fireman Silver, Blotch and Carbon run
in fright upstage, through the trees, which then turn around. We see that they
are not trees at all, but great paper clips disguised. One of the curved surfaces
menacingly goes up and down, and can clearly lasso anyone unfortunate
enough to get close. When Fireman Silver, Blotch and Carbon turn to look
downstage, they only see the "tree" side of the Paperclips, and cannot see
the frightening side in view of the audience. They run between the "trees"
again, and the Paperclips move back without turning round. So Fireman
Silver, Blotch and Carbon, now downstage, can see the Paperclip side for the
first time. They react and try to exit, but too late; at last, Fireman Silver, in
the centre, is lassoed by one of the Paperclips, while Blotch and Carbon*

escape, one each side of the stage, pursued by the other Paperclips. Fireman Silver struggles to pull off the "hoop" surrounding him, Blotch and Carbon enter again and try to rescue Fireman Silver, but the Paperclips catch up with them and off they all chase once more. Blotch and Carbon return a second time, as Fireman Silver enters desperate straits, and this time manage to free him. Then he helps them to manoeuvre all three Paperclips into such a position that they lasso each other. Leaving them struggling, Fireman Silver, Blotch and Carbon escape

The Lights fade

SCENE 2

The River Ink

Over the river hangs the branch of a tree. On the tree a notice says DANGER—DEEP INK. The river itself could be blue silky material. There is no bridge—the only way to cross the river is to place a plank from one side to the other. (NB. If the overhanging branch proves impracticable, a large rock would be fine)

The Salamander drags on a tired Tishoo and flings her down on the bank. He searches around and finds the plank. He appears to have an idea, takes the plank, lifts it above his head and stealthily approaches Tishoo from behind, as if he is going to brain her. The Audience will probably shout a warning. Tishoo turns, and gasps with fright, but the Salamander immediately drops the plank over the river to make a bridge. He is suddenly very polite

Tishoo Atishoo. You were going to knock me out!

The Salamander shakes his head. He mimes hunger

What? You're hungry?

The Salamander shakes his head and points to her

Am *I* hungry?

The Salamander nods

Well, yes. But I'm almost too tired to eat.

The Salamander pats her shoulders sympathetically. We really should believe, with Tishoo, that his warm side is now here to stay

It's a long journey. Atishoo.

The Salamander nods, then, miming to her to wait there, goes behind the tree, and brings out something in his cupped paws

What is it?

The Salamander hands it to her like a present and mimes eating

Well, thank you. (*She relaxes a little as she receives his offering. Then she sees what it is—a large blue frog. She screams as it jumps about*) Aah! It's a frog!

The Salamander appears to laugh as Tishoo finally manages to get rid of it in the river

Atishoo. Atishoo.

Song 10: Burn Me

(*Singing*)   Burn me, burn me
                   Breathe a flame and burn me
                   Please don't play around with me
                   For I can't bear this uncertainty
                   Make your mind up now to set me free
                   Or spurn me
                   And burn me!

                   Burn me, burn me
                   Breathe a flame and burn me
                   Now you're friendly, now you tease
                   And now with terror you make me freeze
                   Make your mind up Salamander please
                   Return me
                   Or burn me!

Burn me, burn me
Breathe a flame and burn me
Yes I'm weak and you are wild
But I'm not meek and I'm not mild
And I won't be treated like a child
Return me
Or burn me!
What a journey!
Just burn me!

The Salamander listens to the song carefully, and shamefacedly goes up to Tishoo and mimes that he can't burn her

(*Speaking*) It's no use trying to get round me. Burn me or leave me alone. Don't play games with me.

The Salamander mimes again. This time she notices

What? You won't burn me?

The Audience may assist Tishoo to interpret the mime

You *can't* burn me?

The Salamander nods mournfully as the truth dawns on her

You mean, after all the panic in Papertown, after all they did to catch you, after all I've been through—you can't breathe fire?

The Salamander nods very sadly. Tishoo laughs

Atishoo. I don't believe it! You're harmless.

The Salamander makes a move towards her

Oh yes. You're stronger than me. But you can't set fire to me. You can't set fire to *anything*. And yet you go around terrifying innocent paper people—(*she is getting hysterical*)—threatening them with the one thing they fear most. I hate you. Why did I try to help you? You didn't deserve it. I hate you. Atishoo.

Tishoo is weeping uncontrollably. Pause. Then the Salamander gently approaches her and puts his arm around her. He, we see, is weeping too. They cry together, then Tishoo recovers, noticing that the Salamander is weeping

I'm sorry. I didn't mean to hurt you.

The Salamander tries to break himself away

It's all right. I won't laugh at you.

The Salamander recovers and mimes an order to cross the river

You want to go on?

The Salamander nods

Then, *please* no more practical jokes. And I won't laugh at you.

The Salamander nods, and helps Tishoo on to the plank

The Salamander and Tishoo cross the river safely and exit. Litterbug enters, laying the Paperchase and following the tracks

Song 10A: The Papertown Paperchase (Reprise)

Litterbug (*unaccompanied*) Litterbug sets the pace
              Of the Papertown Paperchase
              Litter clues I will lay
              So Papertown people can find the way
              Papertown ...

He sees the Audience and breaks off

(*Speaking*) Aha. The River Ink. And the tracks stop this side. (*He screws up his eyes*) There they go again the other side. We'll have to cross the river. (*He crosses on the plank*)

A loud, gleeful giggling is heard. Litterbug turns

The Paperweight, a large round lady, enters, hopping and bouncing along, stamping viciously and with relish on all the pieces of paper Litterbug has dropped

Paperweight Stamp, stamp, stamp. Got you, got you. Crush the paper, crush the paper, stamp, stamp, stamp. (*She sees Litterbug and stops*) Who are you?

Litterbug I'm Litterbug. Who are you?

Song 11: I'm Paperweight

Paperweight   I'm Paperweight
Bumpetty bump
Paperweight
Clumpetty clumpetty clump
Paperweight
Grumpetty grumpetty grump
A great big lumpetty lump.

I'm so stout
If you're made of paper look out
I'm so fat
If you're made of paper I'll squash you flat.

I'm Paperweight
Bumpetty bump
Paperweight
Clumpetty clumpetty clump
Paperweight
Grumpetty grumpetty grump
A great big lumpetty lump.

(*Speaking*) What are you doing here?

Litterbug I'm laying a paperchase.

Paperweight I can see that.

Litterbug And some people are following it.

Paperweight What sort of people?

Litterbug Paper people, of course. We're crossing the river.

Paperweight Paper people?

Litterbug Yes.

Paperweight (*laughing with hysterical delight*) People to stamp on, people to crush, paper people to knock in the river!

Litterbug Wait a minute, you can't do that.

Paperweight Who says? They'll cross the plank and I'll jump on them. (*She climbs to the branch above it*)

Litterbug But. Oh, no. And I can't stop to warn them, I've got to follow the tracks—I'd better leave a message for them—(*noticing the Audience*)—I couldn't leave it with you again could I? Oh, thank you. (*Almost whispering*) Now what shall we tell them? I know. Listen.

Song 11A: The Second Clue

(*Singing*)   Beware, beware,
                   Take great care
                   Not to cross the river on the plank.

Litterbug rehearses the Audience, making sure they don't sing loudly enough for the Paperweight to hear; and bringing them in after a count of three

That's fine. Don't forget. You must all sing the message together, so wait for Fireman Silver to say one, two, three, and then sing. Good luck.

Litterbug begins to exit. Paperweight, from her branch, stops him

Paperweight Are you off, Litterbug?
Litterbug Yes.
Paperweight Will your friends be here soon?
Litterbug I expect so.
Paperweight Oh, goody, goody, goody, good.

Litterbug looks at the Audience with a gesture of "good luck" and exits. A marching version of the "Papertown Paperchase" song heralds the arrival of Fireman Silver, Blotch and Carbon. They march in, straight towards the river and the plank

Fireman Silver March, march, hup, hup, march, march, hup, hup . . . (*Just as they reach the river*) One, (*beat*) two, (*beat*) three . . .

Song 11B: The Second Clue (Reprise)

Audience (*singing*) Beware, beware
                        Take great care
                        Not to cross the river on the plank.

As the Audience sing, Fireman Silver, Blotch and Carbon stop to listen

Blotch Did you just hear something sounding something like another message?

Carbon Yes, it started when Fireman Silver said . . .
Fireman Silver One, (*beat*) two, (*beat*) three . . .
Audience (*singing*) Beware, beware
             Take great care
             Not to cross the river on the plank.
Fireman Silver Is that another message from Litterbug? It is? Well, thank
   you one and all. We are warned not to cross the river on the plank, but the
   Paperchase trail continues the other side. Therefore, we have to cross
   somehow. How?
Blotch (*looking in the river for the first time*) Aaah! INK! (*He begins to shake
   uncontrollably, as though he has shellshock*)
Fireman Silver (*nervous*) Ink?
Carbon So it is. Well, that's all right.
Fireman Silver You know the stories they tell about the Ink Well in
   Papertown. Ink brings death.
Blotch Look at my wound.
Carbon Old wives' tales.
Blotch All I did was drop a paper pellet into the well to see how deep it was.
   And then "splosh." And now I'm scarred for life.
Fireman Silver How come you weren't killed outright?
Blotch I don't know. Luck?
Carbon Luck? I reckon you have a magical resistance to ink.
Blotch What?
Carbon Let's put it to the test. Fireman Silver and I will climb on your back
   and you can wade across.
Blotch (*shaking again*) Oh, no. I couldn't.
Fireman Silver It's your duty. For the sake of Papertown.
Carbon You'll be the bravest blotting paper ever known if you succeed.
Blotch What?
Carbon The bravest.

*Pause. Perhaps Blotch asks the Audience if he should make this supreme
sacrifice*

Blotch (*eventually*) All right. I'll try.
Fireman Silver Brave chap. I won't forget this.

*Gingerly, Blotch enters the ink; the other two straddle him. He slowly but
surely crosses the river; music echoes the tension*

They reach dry land and exit hurriedly. If possible, or certainly by their next entrance, Blotch should have more war wounds—ink blots—on his costume

The Paperweight appears on the branch above (or from behind the rock). She watches, and is furious as they escape

Paperweight Grrrr. I can't reach them! (*She shakes her fist at them and falls into the river. She screams with rage*)

The Lights fade

Scene 3

Scissors Gorge

Night. A spiky, bladelike, murky landscape, with a notice saying "Scissors Gorge". Tishoo and the Salamander are playing Blind Man's Buff. The Salamander wears a handkerchief over his eyes and is trying to find Tishoo, who dodges behind rocks, giggling happily and cupping her hands to create a false echo for her voice. The Salamander is clearly enjoying the game too

Tishoo (*laughing*) You'll never catch me, never catch me. Atishoo. I'm over here!

Tishoo changes her position, running very lightly on her toes. The Salamander is fooled and ends up in the wrong place

Wrong! I'm over *here*, you soppy Salamander. Atishoo.

The Salamander approaches, and this time Tishoo is virtually trapped in a corner. She tries to get past, but his outstretched arms make it impossible

Ah. You're getting warm. Warmer. (*Laughing*) Very warm. Ooh hot, so hot, so *very* hot.

The Salamander grabs her, excited and pleased

I'm burning. Ha, ha...

She stops, realizing what she has said. The Salamander leaves go of her, pulls the blindfold off, and sulkily walks away

I'm sorry. That wasn't a joke. Just part of the game. (*She approaches him tenderly*) I really am sorry. Forgive me?

Pause. Then the Salamander nods. Tishoo is relieved

Thank you. My turn.

She starts to put the blindfold on. The Salamander clearly does not want to play

No? No more to-day? (*He shakes his head*) All right. Atishoo. (*Pause*) Atishoo. (*Pause*) Atishoo.

The Salamander looks up

I'm sorry. Sneezing more than usual. It's so cold here. Atishoo.

The Salamander is concerned. He approaches her and gently puts his arm round her. Then he has an idea; he collects a pile of sticks and lays them on the ground, as if to say "Let's light a fire." Tishoo looks apprehensive

A fire?

The Salamander nods

How will you light it?

The Salamander picks up two sticks and rubs them together. But he has no success

Should I try?

The Salamander shakes his head vehemently

All right.

The Salamander suddenly decides on a firm course of action. He pushes the surprised Tishoo away from the sticks, and prepares, with great concentration, to blow on the fire and, hopefully, light it. He tries once, without success. Then a second time. Tishoo realizes what he is doing and encourages him

Song 11C: Burn It (Reprise)

(Singing)   Burn it, burn it
                 Breathe a flame and burn it
                 Close your eyes and concentrate
                 Prove to me you're not second rate
                 To the Land of Fire return in state
                 You'll earn it
                 Just burn it!
                 Please learn it!
                 Please burn it!

With a huge final effort, the Salamander succeeds. The fire begins to smoke, and soon we see a red glow

You've done it!

The Salamander watches with pride. He puts his arm out to her

Me? I didn't do it.

The Salamander mimes again

You breathed fire for me?

The following section (to p. 53) can be cut if required

Both look at each other, and then excitement takes over. They jump for joy, as the fire happily smokes. Suddenly we hear the voice of Litterbug following the trail, humming "The Papertown Paperchase" song

The mood changes instantly

   *The Salamander picks up Tishoo and exits with her at speed. Litterbug
   enters, humming "The Papertown Paperchase" song and laying his trail*

He stops at the notice, which is quite high. He strains to read it, thus encouraging the Audience to shout out what it says. If they don't take the hint he can ask them to read it for him

Audience Scissors Gorge.

Litterbug Scissors Gorge? Ugh. (*His knees begin to tremble*) I have heard
that Scissors Gorge is the most dangerous place in the world. Still, from the
tracks, it looks as though the Salamander and Tishoo aren't far away. (*He
has an idea*) Can I leave another message with you? Thank you, I ——

*He is stopped by a very nasty regular sound—two blades snapping hungrily
open and shut. His knees tremble, he looks frantically for somewhere to hide,
and finds somewhere just in the nick of time*

*Scissors enters, snapping his blades menacingly. He pauses, looks around,
then exits*

Litterbug reappears to give the message

Quickly, w-w-w-w-w-while w-w-w-w-we have the chance. Please tell
Fireman Silver, Blotch and Carbon . . .

Song 11D: The Third Clue

(*Singing*)   Beware, beware
                   Take great care
                   Carbon is the one to pull you through.

*Litterbug rehearses the Audience, anxiously looking off stage in case
Scissors returns. As he finishes, we hear the snapping blades again, Litterbug
leaps in the air and starts to exit*

Don't forget to wait for the one, two, three . . . Oooooh !

*Litterbug scuttles off, almost forgetting in his fright to scatter litter.
Scissors enters, and menacingly looks around. He notices the paper on the
ground, and very deliberately kicks it away so that the Paperchase trail is
broken. As he exits one side, Fireman Silver, Blotch and Carbon enter the
other. They follow the trail until they realize it has stopped. The Audience
may well shout out, but they take little notice as they search for the next
clue. Without them seeing, Scissors enters menacingly and walks towards
them, they hear the snapping, turn, scream and run off terrified. Scissors
carries on after them. After a pause, Fireman Silver, Blotch and Carbon
nervously appear*

Fireman Silver Now listen, lads. Terrifying that object may be, but there is only one of him. Look how many of us there are. One . . .
Blotch Two.
Carbon Three.

Song 11E: The Third Clue (Reprise)

Audience (*singing*) Beware, beware
                        Take great care
                        Carbon is the one to pull you through.
Fireman Silver They've done it again. Thank you.
Blotch But what did it mean? What can Carbon do?
Fireman Silver Two years. For forgery.
Carbon And my magic.
Fireman Silver (*doubtfully*) What magic?
Carbon Carbon paper magic.
Blotch What's that?
Carbon Like forgery. I can make one thing turn into two, exactly the same.
Fireman Silver How?
Carbon By pressing it against me.
Blotch (*bemused*) Pressing it . . .

Suddenly the snapping blades are heard again

Fireman Silver Quick!

Fireman Silver, Blotch and Carbon huddle together and Fireman Silver whispers his plan. They place Carbon against, or near, a tree. Fireman Silver and Blotch hide

Scissors enters, sees Carbon, and snaps his blades excitedly

Scissors advances on Carbon, who starts reacting terrified. At the right moment, Fireman Silver and Blotch rush out of hiding, grab Scissors and forcibly press him up against Carbon. Tension music builds as they release him, and from behind Carbon emerges an identical pair of Scissors! It sees the first pair and chases it away from Fireman Silver, Blotch and Carbon, who set off on their quest once more, congratulating each other. They find the trail picks up again just before they go

Fireman Silver, Blotch and Carbon exit

To music, the two pairs of Scissors fight a duel until finally they both collapse dead or exhausted

The Lights fade

SCENE 4

Salamander's Cave

It is night time. Tishoo and the Salamander are finishing off a meal of berries, etc., on improvised plates

The optional cut ends here

The Salamander yawns

Song 12: Sleepy Salamander

Tishoo   It's been a long day
But we've come through the worst time
For the first time
You breathed fire, dear
And now you're tired, dear.

You're a sleepy Salamander
Such a sleepy Salamander
It's no surprise, it's no surprise
Go to sleep now Salamander
Let me gently put my hand up-
-on your head
Use my lap for a bed, now
And close your eyes
And close your eyes.

Tonight
It seems

Your troubles may be past
Goodnight
Sweet dreams
I'm glad we're friends at last.

You're a sleepy Salamander
Such a sleepy Salamander
You've done your best, you've done your best
Go to sleep now Salamander
No use trying to withstand a
Weary yawn
Till the dawn brings the morning
It's time to rest
It's time to rest.

By the end of the song, the Salamander is asleep with his head on Tishoo's lap. She very soon dozes off too

Litterbug enters gingerly, sees them asleep, and throws down the last piece of litter for his trail

Litterbug (*whispering*) Aah!

Song 12A: The Papertown Paperchase (Whispered Reprise)

(*Singing*)   At last we're face to face
                   It's the end of the Paperchase
                   Papertown will be free
                   For Papertown people like you and me

Fireman Silver, Blotch and Carbon join in, off, and enter singing

Litterbug,
Fireman Silver,   Papertown people like you and me.
Blotch and   From Papertown
Carbon   Via Paperclip Forest ...

Litterbug indicates to them to be quiet

Litterbug Shhh . . .

Fireman Silver picks up the last piece of litter, looks up and sees the Salamander and Tishoo in the cave

Fireman Silver (*loudly*) There they are!
Litterbug Shhhhhh!
Blotch Are they dead?
Carbon No, they're asleep.
Litterbug What are you going to do?
Fireman Silver (*rather too loudly*) Wake them up.

Tishoo wakes

Tishoo Atishoo.

This wakes the Salamander, who lifts his head, sensing something is wrong. The others freeze

Did you hear something?
Fireman Silver It's us, Miss Tishoo, Fireman Silver.

The Salamander leaps up to protect Tishoo. He starts breathing heavily, as if preparing to attack

Tishoo (*to the Salamander*) It's all right. He won't hurt me. (*To Fireman Silver*) What do you want?
Fireman Silver We have engaged upon this quest, Miss Tishoo, at the request of the Papertown Council to escort the Salamander back to his home—the Land of Fire.
Tishoo I'm sure the Salamander would love to go home. Wouldn't you?

The Salamander nods but then sadly shakes his head

What's the matter? You *don't* want to go home?

He shakes his he 'again

Why not?

The Salamander mimes breathing fire, etc.

Oh, I see.

Fireman Silver Kindly interpret, Miss Tishoo.
Tishoo He was instructed to burn down Papertown—and he hasn't.
Carbon Well, I suggest a little white lie.
Tishoo What do you mean?
Carbon Well, we'll all say he *has* burnt it down.
Fireman Silver It's worth a try. Though I don't like telling lies.
Blotch (*whispering*) It's for the good of Papertown.
Tishoo (*to the Salamander*) Well, what do you say?

The Salamander shakes his head

Fireman Silver He must!
Tishoo Shh. Please, Fireman Silver.

Tishoo takes the Salamander on one side

(*To the Salamander*) Listen. Earlier tonight you proved to me that you could really breathe fire. Yes?

The Salamander nods

You can do it again. Can't you? In the Land of Fire?

The Salamander nods

Then there's no need to burn down Papertown—my home. Please.

Pause. The Salamander nods

Thank you. (*To the others*) He'll come.
Fireman Silver Oh well done, Miss Tishoo. Forward — to the Land of Fire.

Music as they journey around the stage. After they have circled once, a red glow appears in the distance

Fireman Silver There it is!

They circle again. The glow is getting brighter

Blotch Fireman Silver, it's getting too hot.
Carbon I'm roasting!
Fireman Silver You two can fall out. Wait for us to return.

Blotch and Carbon stop, and exit

The others continue, circling the stage, reacting to the heat getting nearer

The music continues. The red glow gets brighter

Litterbug Fireman Silver. I can't go on. I'm burning.
Fireman Silver Very well. Fall out, Litterbug.

Litterbug stops, and exits

The others continue, circling once more, reacting to the increasing heat

The music continues. The red glow gets brighter. Tishoo stumbles, nearly fainting. The Salamander helps her up, concerned

Fireman Silver Miss Tishoo! You'd better not come any further.
Tishoo All right! Good luck.

Tishoo leaves, waving

Fireman Silver leads the Salamander round again

The glow gets even brighter. They reach the Land of Fire

SCENE 5

The Entrance to the Land of Fire

Fireman Silver rings the bell by means of a large bellrope. Two Fireflies emerge, and then the Chief Firefly. The Salamander bows; he is clearly very nervous

Chief Firefly Why, it's the Salamander!
Firefly 1 Sal—
Firefly 2   —a—
Firefly 1   —man—
Firefly 2   —der.
Chief Firefly Have you succeeded? Have you burnt down Papertown?

Before the Salamander can answer, Fireman Silver interrupts

Fireman Silver Yes, sir. He has indeed. To the ground.
Chief Firefly And who are you?
Fireman Silver Silver's the name, sir, Fireman of Papertown.
Chief Firefly And you say he has carried out my orders?
Fireman Silver (*not easily*) Yes, sir. Papertown is no more.
Chief Firefly I do not believe you. If Papertown is destroyed, how come you are here? You are paper, are you not, Fireman Silver? Very well, then. I need further proof of the Salamander's fire-breathing ability. (*To the Salamander*) You will burn this fireman. (*To the Fireflies*) Seize him!

The Fireflies hold Fireman Silver

Fireman Silver (*breaking free*) He can't burn me.
Chief Firefly (*stopping*) Why not?
Fireman Silver Because I am made of silver paper; silver paper does not burn.
Chief Firefly (*to the Audience*) Is this true?
Audience Yes.
Fireman Silver So take my word for it, sir. He *can* breathe fire.
Chief Firefly Take your word? No. I will find another test for him.

Tishoo enters, hot and exhausted, dragged by two Fireflies

The Salamander reacts

Firefly 3 Chief Firefly, we found this creature acting suspiciously.
Fireman Silver Tishoo!
Chief Firefly You know this creature?
Fireman Silver Yes, she's Tishoo, a paper tissue.
Chief Firefly Paper?
Fireman Silver (*aware of what he has done*) Yes.
Chief Firefly Salamander. Burn Tishoo.

The Salamander looks horror struck. Music for tension

This is your last chance. Fail and you will be banished forever.
Fireflies FOREVER!

Song 13: Burn Her (Reprise)

Chief Firefly   Burn her, burn her
Breathe a flame and burn her
Prove your place back here you've earned
By showing us what you say you've learned
To a cinder we want Tishoo burned
So burn her!
Yes burn her!
Go on burn her!
Just burn her!

Music for tension as the Salamander prepares to breathe fire. He builds up his breathing; but at the last moment, courage fails him and he runs to Tishoo and hugs her, weeping hysterically. Tishoo holds him to her. The Fireflies hiss with displeasure

Chief Firefly Silence! Fireflies, leave us.

The Fireflies exit

Salamander.

The Salamander nervously steps forward. Drum roll for tension

You are a traitor. You have joined with our enemies, and brought disgrace to the Land of Fire. I hereby declare war on Papertown. You, Salamander, will fight or you will die. Your "friends" — (*he sneers*) — will return and prepare Papertown for invasion. I will not rest until Papertown is destroyed. Come.

The Salamander slowly goes in, looking sadly at Tishoo and Fireman Silver. He exits with the Chief Firefly

Tishoo and Fireman Silver look at each other and quickly decide they must hurry back to Papertown. They set off around the stage, accompanied by silent-film music and lighting. At certain points of their journey they pick up Blotch, Carbon, and Litterbug, where they had left them. All then hurry towards Papertown, perhaps running on the spot, facing downstage, in slow motion

Meanwhile, the set changes behind them. When the set change is complete:

All Clear the streets! The Fireflies are coming.

The Lights come up on:

SCENE 6

Papertown Square

A siren blares out

Fireman Silver, Tishoo, Litterbug, Carbon and Blotch "arrive" and start spreading the news. Fireman Silver blows his whistle to attract attention

The Postman and Mr Quid enter and meet the others

Lady Carrier Bag enters on her bicycle. She nearly falls off. Mr Quid dashes into the bank

Fireman Silver sends Litterbug to keep look-out, then knocks on the bookshop door

Fireman Silver
Tishoo   } *(together)* Clear the streets! The Fireflies are coming!
Carbon   } *etc.*
Blotch

Spike enters and distributes silver paper fire hats; everyone receives one except the Postman

Professor Paperback opens his door, receives the news and brings out his special books to protect them

Mr Quid emerges from the bank carrying money-bags. He, Professor Paperback and Lady Carrier Bag take shelter in the Town Hall

Lady Carrier Bag Good luck, Fireman Silver. Papertown relies on you!
Fireman Silver Aye aye, ma'am. This way, lads.

Fireman Silver, Blotch and Carbon exit, passing the Postman, who is still waiting for a hat

Clear the streets, Postman!

The Postman exits, passing Spike, who has only one hat left but does not give it to the Postman

Spike (*seeing Tishoo and moving to her*) Go home, Tishoo.
Tishoo No.
Spike You'll burn.
Tishoo He won't burn anyone if I can talk to him.
Spike But what about the fireflies?

Tishoo exits, pursued by Spike

Fireman Silver, Blotch and Carbon enter, carrying sand buckets

The Postman, returning, still in search of a hat, meets Fireman Silver's party

Fireman Silver CLEAR THE STREETS! Out of the way, Postman. Buckets, lads!

The Postman scuttles into the Town Hall. Blotch and Carbon find fire buckets

Carbon There must be an easier way to fight fire than with sand.
Fireman Silver Nonsense. Throw sand on a flame and it goes out instantly.
Carbon There must be something better for tackling big fires.

The audience may shout out "water", in which case the answer is "No water in Papertown". At any rate the audience should be encouraged to suggest ink from the Ink Well

Blotch Ink? From the Ink Well? Impossible.
Fireman Silver We can't use that—remember it's said someone will die there.
Carbon Oh come on, it's worth a try. Blotch, you can't be afraid of ink any more?

Blotch Oh very well, Fireman Silver.
Fireman Silver All right, lads. Fill the buckets.

Blotch and Carbon fill buckets from the Ink Well during the following

Litterbug dashes in, breathless

Litterbug They're coming, they're coming!
Fireman Silver How long have we got?
Litterbug A few minutes at the most.
Fireman Silver Back to your post!

Litterbug exits

Blotch and Carbon finish filling the buckets during the following

Fireman Silver Everything ready?
Blotch
Carbon } *(together)* Nearly, Fireman Silver.
Fireman Silver Right, to work— (*He sees the audience*) Wait a minute.
What about all these citizens here? How are they going to defend
themselves.
Carbon May I make a suggestion, Fireman Silver?
Fireman Silver Permission granted.
Carbon If they have something silver to hold up and shine at the Fireflies,
they won't get burnt.
Fireman Silver Good idea. Something silver. Have you all got something
silver? A coin? A piece of silver paper from your chocolate? Or the back
of a badge? Quickly, have a look. Anybody *not* got something silver? All
those without, share with those with!

*Blotch and Carbon could hand out silver objects, perhaps chocolate coins or
milk bottle tops to those in the audience who have none*

Let's have a practice. When I give the command, I want you all to hold your
silver objects in the air. Blotch and Carbon, you pretend to be Fireflies.

Blotch and Carbon hide

Ready everyone? Fireflies forward!

Blotch and Carbon appear, pretending to be Fireflies

Silver objects raise! Now!

Blotch and Carbon react

Excellent, citizens. Put them down and wait for my command later. Good luck!

Blotch Fireman Silver, I've got an idea. How they could help *us*.

Fireman Silver Go ahead, but make it brief.

Blotch Fireflies hate anything wet. Now we haven't got very much ink in the well. Supposing everybody pretended it was raining, the Fireflies might be fooled.

Fireman Silver Excellent. So what do they do?

Blotch When you blow your whistle, they could make noises like a storm.

Fireman Silver Of course! Now first let's practise thunder. First a clap.

The audience is encouraged to clap

Now the thunder.

The audience is encouraged to stamp their feet

And then the rain.

The audience is encouraged to make noises like rain—pitter, patter, pitter, patter, etc.

Now let's put it all together. Wait for the whistle before we begin.

The audience is rehearsed, with the whistle: clap, then thunder, then rain

Excellent. Now listen to me, citizens. These noises are only to be used in emergency. When I blow the whistle and not before. When I blow the whistle. But keep your silver objects handy all the time.

Litterbug enters

Litterbug They're here. They're here. (*He jumps up and down, scattering litter*)

Fireman Silver Control, Litterbug, control. (*To the Audience*) Good luck, citizens.

The fire siren blares as everybody hides. Music

The Chief Firefly, the Salamander and four Fireflies enter and look savagely around. The Chief Firefly points out his instructions, sending several Fireflies and the Salamander off

Two Fireflies are left, and begin to burn down the Town with their flaming torches

The Chief Firefly exits. Fireman Silver enters cautiously, followed by Blotch and Carbon carrying their buckets.

At first they fail to see the Fireflies but, guided by the audience ——

Dialogue (if necessary)

Blotch
Carbon } (*together*) Where are they?
Audience Behind you!

—throw the buckets of ink on the Fireflies and chase them off, the Fireflies hissing with pain

A Firefly enters, looks around surreptitiously and tiptoes to a building. Spike enters, sees him and as he bends to set fire to the wall, spikes him in the rear and chases him off

Two Fireflies enter with the Salamander and order him to burn something. He looks reluctant. They become angry, whereupon he turns viciously on them and chases them off

Tishoo, who has seen the last episode, comes on and makes to follow the Salamander. A Firefly enters behind her. In spite of audience reaction she fails to see him

Just as the Firefly is about to pounce, Litterbug runs on, nips in front of the Firefly on all fours, and kneels crouched in front of him. The Firefly trips over him, Litterbug tickles him while Tishoo escapes. Litterbug runs off and the Firefly, still recovering from his shock, exits in the other direction

The Chief Firefly meets the exiting Firefly and drags him back. Two other Fireflies also enter

Chief Firefly Where is the Salamander?

Firefly 1 (*nervously*) We have lost him, Chief Firefly.

Chief Firefly Lost him? (*Furiously*) We are being made fools of. *Why?*

Firefly 2 (*indicating the Audience*) All these citizens are foiling our efforts. They keep warning Papertown the moment they see us trying to burn anything.

Chief Firefly What? (*Turning on the Audience*) I'll teach you to make me look silly. Fireflies, burn them all!

The Fireflies prepare for battle

Fireman Silver rushes on

Fireman Silver (*to the Audience*) Silver objects raise, now!

The Audience do so and the Fireflies react in dismay. They are powerless and shy away, defeated (including the Chief Firefly)

(*To the Audience*) Well done, citizens!

Blotch and Carbon enter with empty buckets

Refill the buckets!

Blotch and Carbon start refilling the buckets from the Ink Well

Unseen by the others, two Fireflies enter

The Fireflies surreptitiously empty the buckets. As soon as another one is filled and put down, they empty it. In spite of Audience reaction, Blotch and Carbon are unaware of this. The Fireflies then stalk Fireman Silver, Blotch and Carbon, who suddenly see them, rush for the buckets, throw the contents —but find there is nothing to throw. Terrified, they run away, but are pinned by the Fireflies against a wall. In desperation, Fireman Silver blows his whistle

Fireman Silver (*to the Audience*) STORM NOW.

The Audience make their pre-rehearsed noises, unnerving the Fireflies, who scatter in fright, pursued by Blotch and Carbon, and finally Fireman Silver who shouts a grateful "Thank you" to the Audience

Tishoo enters, still looking for the Salamander

Unseen by Tishoo, the Chief Firefly approaches and grabs her from behind

Spike enters, sees what has happened, and rushes to help

In the ensuing struggle Spike is pushed aside, falls and hurts himself. He lies clutching his leg. The Chief Firefly prepares to carry Tishoo off

In the nick of time the Salamander enters, sees his friend Tishoo in difficulty, and savagely goes for the Chief Firefly

The Chief Firefly, frightened, drops Tishoo, who runs to help Spike. The Chief Firefly and the Salamander stage an exciting duel, circling each other and then fighting. Eventually the Salamander forces the Chief Firefly up against the Ink Well, then over the side and into it. Blue smoke rises from the Ink Well as the Chief Firefly is extinguished. Cheers of congratulation, as Tishoo leaves Spike, who has virtually recovered, and greets the Salamander warmly

Litterbug rushes on delighted, followed by Fireman Silver, who looks down the Well to see that the Chief Firefly is no more

Tishoo Well done. Thank you.
Spike Congratulations, Salamander. You were very brave.
Litterbug We've won! We've won! (*He scatters litter with joy*)
Fireman Silver Control, Litterbug. (*Coming from the Ink Well*) Thank you Salamander, sir, the Chief Firefly is well and truly extinguished.

Blotch and Carbon enter, escorting two sheepish Fireflies

Carbon All the other Fireflies have fled, Fireman Silver.
Blotch And these two can go in the Waste-Paper Basket!

Lady Carrier Bag, Professor Paperback, Mr Quid and the Postman enter from the Town Hall

Lady Carrier Bag Is it safe? We heard cheering.
Fireman Silver Councillors. Papertown has been saved from the threat of fire.
Lady Carrier Bag Oh splendid.
Professor Paperback Thank you.
Lady Carrier Bag Fireman Silver, the Council gratefully awards you the Papertown Star of Honour.

Applause. Fireman Silver steps forward and is decorated

Professor Paperback In recognition of their loyalty and bravery, which we respect as a sign of their reformed characters, Blotch and Carbon ——

Blotch and Carbon step forward

—— are to be released and set free.

Cheers. Blotch and Carbon return to guard their Firefly captives

Mr Quid To express our thanks to Litterbug ——

Litterbug steps forward

—— we intend to reward him —— er, not with money —— with the freedom of Papertown.
Litterbug Thank you, Mr Quid. What does that mean?
Mr Quid It means you can come and go as you please and scatter as much litter as you like.
Litterbug Well, thank you, but scattering litter seems to get me into too many scrapes. But there's no reason why I shouldn't ...
Mr Quid What?
Litterbug From now on I shall collect litter instead and help Spike the Pen keep Papertown tidy.

Cheers. Litterbug starts picking up litter and cramming it into his bag

Fireman Silver Permission to speak, your Ladyship?
Lady Carrier Bag Granted.

Fireman Silver I would like to point out that without the actions of one brave creature, our plan might not have met with such success.
Lady Carrier Bag Indeed. Salamander, kindly step forward.

Song 14: Salute the Salamander

All   Salute the Salamander
                            He served us with distinction
                            Salute the Salamander
                            He saved us from extinction.

                            Salute the Salamander
                            He acted like a hero
                            Salute the Salamander
                            His cowardice is zero.

                            His courage never swerves
                            His exploits seldom fail
                            A medal he deserves
                            We'll pin it on his tail.

                            Salute the Salamander
                            His scales are quite unbroken
                            Salute the Salamander
                            Accept this as a token
                            Of esteem and renown
                            Salute the Salamander
                            The saviour of Papertown.

Lady Carrier Bag We thank you and would like to reward you with whatever you desire.
Mr Quid (*nervously*) Money ?

The Salamander shakes his head

Professor Paperback Perhaps you would like to stay here and live with us?

The Salamander shakes his head

Lady Carrier Bag Then how can we say thank you?

The Salamander mimes that he wants to go home to the Land of Fire

Tishoo Home? To the Land of Fire?
Lady Carrier Bag But that seems such a simple request.
Tishoo I think he's homesick, aren't you?

The Salamander nods. The Two Fireflies rush forward and prostrate themselves before Lady Carrier Bag

Firefly 1 Please let us speak.
Firefly 2 Have mercy and hear us.
Lady Carrier Bag Very well.
Firefly 1 On behalf of all the Fireflies in the Land of Fire, we want to say we're sorry.
Firefly 2 The Chief Firefly forced us to obey him. We are glad he has been extinguished.
Firefly 1 If the Salamander returns we would like *him* to be our Chief and lead us wisely and peacefully.
Firefly 2 Then we would never threaten Papertown again.
Lady Carrier Bag Seems reasonable. What do you say, Salamander?

The Salamander nods his head. The two Fireflies bow to him

Lady Carrier Bag Very well. (*To the Fireflies*) I will release you. Take care of your new leader and live in peace, as we hope to do.

Music: the Salamander says good-bye to each character individually. Finally he goes to Tishoo and embraces her. All wave good-bye

The Salamander leaves, flanked by the two Fireflies

Tishoo returns sadly to Spike, who comforts her

All turn to the audience

All (*singing*)   Town of paper buildings
                              Town of paper people

There's a paper church
With a paper steeple.
All is safe, all is sound
All's well in Papertown.

All take up frozen positions as ——

—— *the* CURTAIN *falls*

FURNITURE AND PROPERTY LIST

The sets given here are suggestions only. It may be easier and more effective to stage the play more simply

ACT I

SCENE 1

On stage: Red hot cave

Off stage: Burning staff (**Chief Firefly**)
Stepping stones (**Fireflies**)
Sticks (**Fireflies**)

SCENE 2

On stage: Ink Well
Bank flat
Bookshop flat
Town Hall flat
2 fire buckets
Litter

Off stage: Sack of mail (**Postman**)
Bicycle (**Lady Carrier Bag**)
Bag of toffees (**Lady Carrier Bag**)
Bag of litter (**Litterbug**)
Litter spike and bag (**Spike**)
Shopping basket (**Tishoo**)

Personal: **Mr Quid:** cigar
Town Crier: watch
Lady Carrier Bag: keys
Fireman Silver: whistle

SCENE 3

On stage: Table. *On it:* papers, pens, dressing
              5 small chairs

SCENE 4

On stage: 3 "paperclip trees"
              Stumps

Off stage: Map **(Postman)**

SCENE 5

On stage: Large wicker basket on rope with crank and handle
              Playing cards set inside basket
              Alarm bell

Off stage: "Hot food trail"—3 dishes of dates cut up small **(Lady
              Carrier Bag,Tishoo, Professor)**
              First Aid Box **(Tishoo)**
              Scarf **(Fireman Silver)**
              Plate of food **(Tishoo)**

SCENE 6

On stage: As Scene 4

SCENE 7

On stage: As Scene 3

ACT II

SCENE I

On stage: As Act I SCENE 4

SCENE 2

On stage: Overhanging tree branch
River banks with "Danger—Deep Ink" notice
Plank
Tree with blue frog hidden behind it

SCENE 3

On stage: Spiky, blade-like cut-out rocks and trees
Notice: "Scissors Gorge"
Small sticks

Personal: **Salamander:** handkerchief

SCENE 4

On stage: 2 stumps
2 plates of berries

SCENE 5

On stage: Gateway flat with bellrope and alarm bell

SCENE 6

On stage: As ACT I Scene 2

Off stage: Box of books **(Professor Paperback)**
Silver paper hats **(All Papertown inhabitants)**
Buckets of "ink" **(Fireman Silver, Blotch, Carbon)**
Bag of silver objects—chocolate coins, milk-bottle tops, etc.
    (Blotch, Carbon)
"Flaming torches" **(Fireflies)**
Medal **(Lady Carrier Bag)**

LIGHTING PLOT

Practical fittings required: fireglow effect in Act II Scene 3

Various interior and exterior settings

ACT I

To open: Glowing Land of Fire lighting

Cue 1	The **Chief Firefly** exits	(Page 5)
	Lights alter for scene change, then fade	
Cue 2	**Salamander** exits	(Page 5)
	Bring up Papertown Square lighting	
Cue 3	Fire siren	(Page 11)
	Cross-fade to Town Hall Council Chamber lighting	
Cue 4	End of "Hot Food Trail" song	(Page 18)
	Cross-fade lights to Waste-Paper Basket	
Cue 5	**Salamander** exits	(Page 20)
	Cross-fade lights to Waste-Paper Basket	
Cue 6	**Tishoo** exits	(Page 26)
	Dim lights slowly throughout rest of scene	
Cue 7	**Spike** exits	(Page 32)
	Cross-fade lights to Paperclip Forest	
Cue 8	**Salamander** carries **Tishoo** off	(Page 34)
	Cross-fade lights to Waste-Paper Basket	

ACT II

To open: Paperclip Forest lighting

Cue 9   **Fireman Silver, Blotch** and **Carbon** escape   (Page 41)
           Cross-fade lights to River Ink

Cue 10   **Paperweight** screams with rage   (Page 48)
           Cross-fade lights to Scissors Gorge; night, murky,
           with red spot concealed beneath sticks

Cue 11   **Salamander** succeeds in breathing fire   (Page 50)
           Bring up red spot to flickering glow

Cue 12   **Scissors** collapses   (Page 53)
           Cross-fade lights to Salamander's cave

Cue 13   **Fireman Silver** et al. journey round the stage   (Page 56)
           Bring up red glow

Cue 14   **Fireman Silver**: "There it is!"   (Page 56)
           Glow gets brighter

Cue 15   **Fireman Silver** et al. circle the stage   (Page 57)
           Glow gets brighter

Cue 16   **Fireman Silver** leads **Salamander** around   (Page 57)
           Glow gets even brighter

Cue 17   They arrive at the entrance to the Land of Fire   (Page57)
           Bring up lights on entrance

Cue 18   **Tishoo** and **Fireman Silver** set off   (Page 59)
           Silent-film lighting

Cue 19   **All**: "The Fireflies are coming."   (Page 60)
           Cross-fade to general lighting on Papertown Square

EFFECTS PLOT

ACT I

ACT II

Cue 12	**Blotch** enters the ink *Tension music*	(Page 47)
Cue 13	**Salamander** lights fire *Smoke effect from twigs*	(Page 50)
Cue 14	**Scissors** advances on **Carbon** *Tension music, building*	(Page 52)
Cue 15	**Fireman Silver:** " ... to the Land of Fire." *Journey music*	(Page 56)
Cue 16	**Chief Firefly:** "Burn Tishoo." *Tension music*	(Page 58)
Cue 17	**Chief Firefly:** " Just burn her!" *Tension music*	(Page 59)
Cue 18	**Chief Firefly:** "Salamander." *Drum roll*	(Page 59)
Cue 19	**Tishoo** and **Fireman Silver** set off *Silent-film music*	(Page 59)
Cue 20	Lights come up on Papertown Square *Fire siren*	(Page 60)
Cue 21	**Fireman Silver:** "Good luck, citizens." *Fire siren; music*	(Page 64)
Cue 22	**Chief Firefly** falls into well *Blue smoke*	(Page 66)

PRINTED IN GREAT BRITAIN BY
THE LONGDUNN PRESS LTD., BRISTOL.